100
Books to
Live By

First published in Great Britain in 2025 by
Michael O'Mara Books Limited
9 Lion Yard
Tremadoc Road
London SW4 7NQ

EU representative:
Authorised Rep Compliance Ltd
Ground Floor, 71 Baggot Street Lower
Dublin D02 P593
Ireland

Copyright © Michael O'Mara Books Limited 2025

All rights reserved. You may not copy, store, distribute, transmit, reproduce or otherwise make available this publication (or any part of it) in any form, or by any means (electronic, digital, optical, mechanical, photocopying, recording, machine readable, text/data mining or otherwise), without the prior written permission of the publisher. Any person who does any unauthorized act in relation to this publication may be liable to criminal prosecution and civil claims for damages.

A CIP catalogue record for this book is available from the British Library.

This product is made of material from well-managed, FSC®-certified forests and other controlled sources. The manufacturing processes conform to the environmental regulations of the country of origin.

For further information see
www.mombooks.com/about/sustainability-climate-focus
Report any safety issues to product.safety@mombooks.com and see
www.mombooks.com/contact/product-safety

UK editions:
ISBN: 978-1-78929-820-8 in hardback print format
ISBN: 978-1-78929-822-2 in ebook format

US editions:
ISBN: 978-1-78929-885-7 in hardback print format
ISBN: 978-1-78929-913-7 in ebook format

1 2 3 4 5 6 7 8 9 10

Cover, design and typeset by Claire Cater, using illustrations from Shutterstock
Printed and bound by CPI Group (UK) Ltd, Croydon, CR0 4YY
www.mombooks.com

100 Books to Live By

LITERARY REMEDIES FOR ANY OCCASION

JOSEPH PIERCY

Michael O'Mara Books Limited

For Polly

Contents

---◆---

Introduction: What Is Bibliotherapy?	6
1. Remedies for the Heart	**11**
2. Remedies for the Soul and Spirit	**55**
3. Remedies for the Mind	**91**
4. Remedies for the Self and Others	**135**
5. Remedies for Everyday Living	**175**
List of Books and Authors	221

---◆---

INTRODUCTION:
What Is Bibliotherapy?

In a world often overwhelmed by the chaos of daily life, where stress, grief and uncertainty can weigh heavily on the human spirit, there exists a quiet, transformative remedy that has been accessible to many yet remains underappreciated: reading. Bibliotherapy, the practice of using literature as a tool for emotional and psychological healing, offers a unique pathway to self-discovery and solace. Through the pages of a book, readers can find mirrors to their own struggles, windows into unfamiliar experiences, and companions in characters. This book explores the profound healing power of reading, delving into how stories can mend broken hearts, soothe troubled minds, and guide us toward greater understanding of ourselves and others.

The concept of bibliotherapy is not new; it has ancient roots, tracing back to the great libraries of ancient Greece, where inscriptions over the entrances declared them as 'healing places for the soul'. Over centuries, literature has served as a refuge for the weary, a space where individuals could confront their fears, process trauma, or simply escape into a world kinder than their own. In the twentieth century, bibliotherapy emerged as a formal practice, employed by librarians, therapists and educators to support mental health and personal growth. The term bibliotherapy was first coined in 1916 by American essayist Samuel McChord Crothers and used to describe the work of the Library War Service during World War I. Traumatized, shell-shocked soldiers returning home were prescribed reading lists to help process the post-traumatic stress. Today, as science increasingly validates the therapeutic benefits of reading – such as reducing stress hormones and lowering blood pressure – this age-old practice is gaining renewed attention as a powerful, accessible form of self-care.

At its core, bibliotherapy operates on the principle that stories have the power to connect us to universal human experiences, reminding us that we are not alone in our pain or joy. Modern research by psychologists, including a pioneering research project by the *Annual Review of Psychology*, has detected identical stimulation in areas of the brain from patients when reading about an experience as when experiencing the same situation in real life. When we read, we engage in a dialogue with the text, interpreting its meaning through the lens of our own lives, which can lead to profound insights and emotional release. Whether it's a novel that helps us grieve a loss by showing us characters who endure similar pain, or a memoir that validates our struggles with mental illness, books can act as gentle guides, helping us navigate the complexities of our inner worlds.

Moreover, bibliotherapy is not a one-size-fits-all approach; it is deeply personal and infinitely adaptable. A child grappling with bullying might find strength in a tale of resilience, while an adult facing burnout could discover renewal in reflective poetry. From curated reading lists used in clinical settings to the spontaneous comfort found in a favourite novel, bibliotherapy can be both structured and organic, meeting individuals where they are in their healing journey.

People see different things in different books and interpret stories from different perspectives. What struck me in the process of compiling this book, however, was how universal many of the themes are, crossing centuries and different cultures throughout history. Care was taken to try to add an international flavour to the list of works offered up as therapy, but what was interesting was how many of the big themes of love, loss, redemption and personal growth are found in all continents and epochs – we are all human and books tell us what it is to be human. For this reason topics such as the search for identity and self-development, or how to cope with a changing world, pop up frequently even when a book is mainly addressing a different issue.

The list of titles in this book is far from exhaustive and only really scratches the surface of how books can help to heal and soothe troubled souls, as the ancient Greeks believed, but it is hoped it illuminates some of the diverse ways in which reading can serve as a balm for the human spirit, offering readers tools to harness literature's restorative potential in their own lives.

What is it about certain texts that resonate so deeply, stitching together the fragmented pieces of our hearts and minds? This book seeks not only to suggest answers to such questions but also to empower you to build your own library of healing, where each volume becomes a stepping stone toward greater compassion, connection and personal growth. Alongside classic and timeless novels are examples of contemporary fiction from around the world and a sprinkling of memoirs and non-fiction. I have also identified what I have named as 'medicine cabinet essentials'; these are works which I believe have universal themes about human life and offer essential values and enrichment. In the entries ahead, we will uncover the magic of words and stories as medicine and therapy, showing how the simple act of reading certain books can transform pain into understanding, isolation into belonging, and silence into a voice that speaks our truth.

Joseph Piercy

1

Remedies for the Heart

CONDITION OR SITUATION:
Losing Faith in Love

PRESCRIPTION:
The Master and Margarita (1967)
by Mikhail Bulgakov

*'Just like a murderer jumps out of nowhere
in an alley, love jumped out in front of
us and struck us both at once.'*

This riotous Russian novel is a mixture of fantasy, philosophy and reflections on society during Stalin's rule. The Master is a struggling writer who has become disillusioned by social pressures and censorship, and feels creatively stifled when his novel is rejected by the Soviet literary establishment. He is, however, loyally supported by his married lover, Margarita, who encourages him to continue his work.

When the Devil arrives in Moscow with an entourage of supernatural beings, he starts to wreak havoc on the literary and intellectual elite of city. Margarita makes a pact with him, ensuring the Master's safety, in return for hosting a surreal and magical ball to which all Moscow's leading figures are invited in order to confront their own moral and philosophical failings. The ball becomes the backdrop for a series of events that highlight the hypocrisy and corruption of Soviet society.

The novel explores the power of love and devotion, shown by Margarita's steadfast belief in the Master's writing as she helps him to be courageous and continue his work despite the rejection and criticism.

Bulgakov also uses the unconventional relationship between the Master and Margarita and their refusal to comply with social norms to highlight Soviet society's emphasis on materialism and ideological conformity. Their love represents individual freedom and creativity that cannot be controlled or suppressed, suggesting that love is a basic human need that cannot be destroyed, however oppressive the society.

Margarita shows selfless devotion to her lover and is willing to make sacrifices for his sake; he in turn finds inspiration for his art through his love for her. Their deep connection is portrayed as spiritual as well as physical, enabling them to communicate intuitively, and Bulgakov demonstrates how powerful and enduring love is.

Alternative Remedy:
Another satire from Soviet-era Russia that is highly critical of post-revolutionary communism is *The Twelve Chairs* (1928) by Ilf and Petrov – a cult classic, there is a conspiracy theory that Bulgakov wrote the novel under a pseudonym.

CONDITION OR SITUATION:
Unrequited Love

PRESCRIPTION:
The Sorrows of Young Werther (1774)
by Johann Wolfgang von Goethe

*'Sometimes I don't understand how another can
love her, is allowed to love her, since I love her
so completely myself, so intensely, so fully, grasp
nothing, know nothing, have nothing but her!'*

Unrequited love is a subject that has inspired literature since time immemorial. Yet when infatuation becomes so all-consuming that it reaches obsessive and damaging depths, it veers into the realm of mania. Before falling into that dark abyss, take a deep breath and reflect with a book.

Few novels have explored the descent into madness caused by unrequited love quite as intensely as *The Sorrows of Young Werther*. This epistolary novel consists of letters written by Werther, describing his travels and his obsession with a young woman. He is an idealist, a romantic anti-hero who falls in love with Charlotte, a woman engaged to another man. Through the course of the novel, Werther's letters become more and more desperate as the pain of his intolerable longing increases – prompting a sudden intervention by a fictional editor/publisher who provides context for Werther's mental decline.

This sudden interjection by a third-person narrator allows the reader to glimpse the effect of Werther's infatuation with Charlotte. At one point, Charlotte gently suggests to Werther that it is the impossibility of him ever consummating his love for her that drives his manic desire, not true love. In this sense the sheer intensity of Werther's passion places tremendous emotional pressures upon Charlotte. The reader has only had Werther's side of the story up until this point, and, at the end of the novel, Goethe intimates that Charlotte's life was blighted by guilt and grief over Werther's fate.

The Sorrows of Young Werther can be read as a novel about mental health, but also as a cautionary tale of the damaging effects of obsessive love, not only on the person who suffers unrequited love, but also on the object of their infatuation.

Alternative Remedies:

The Sorrows of Young Werther is a heartbreaking tragedy, so for patients wishing to avoid emotional side effects, *Like Water for Chocolate* (1989) by Mexican writer Laura Esquivel can illuminate longing from a magical realism perspective. For a gentle evocation of the enduring power of regret try *On Chesil Beach* (2007) by Ian McEwan.

CONDITION OR SITUATION:
Fear of Following One's Heart's Desires

PRESCRIPTION:
A Room with a View (1908)
by E. M. Forster

> *'It is so difficult – at least I find it difficult – to understand people who speak the truth.'*

E. M. Forster's classic novel, set in the early twentieth century, explores themes of love, social convention and personal awakening. The story follows Lucy Honeychurch, a young Englishwoman from a respectable family, as she embarks on a journey of self-discovery. The novel begins during her chaperoned trip to Florence with her older cousin, Charlotte Bartlett. There Lucy meets the unconventional Emerson family – George Emerson, a passionate and free-spirited young man, and his father, an eccentric socialist.

A spontaneous kiss between Lucy and George stirs her emotions, challenging her sheltered upbringing. Upon returning to England, Lucy becomes engaged to Cecil Vyse, a cultured but emotionally stifling man who represents the rigid bounds of her class. As Lucy grapples with her feelings for George and the constraints of Edwardian society, she must decide whether to follow her heart or conform to the expectations imposed upon her. The novel culminates in a choice that reflects her personal growth and desire for authentic love over propriety.

A Room with a View contrasts genuine emotional connection with the repressive social norms of Edwardian England. Lucy's attraction to George represents raw, unbridled passion, while her engagement to Cecil symbolizes societal expectation and emotional restraint. Forster also exposes the hypocrisy of Edwardian society, where outward propriety often masks inner discontent. The story critiques the rigid class structure of the time, particularly through the contrast between the middle-class Honeychurch family and the unconventional, lower-middle-class Emersons. Characters like Cecil and Charlotte embody the repression and superficiality that Lucy ultimately rejects in favour of spontaneity and being true to one's desires.

Lucy's relationship with George transforms her worldview, allowing her to shed the repressive values of her upbringing. Love across class barriers becomes a catalyst for personal growth, teaching readers that such relationships can challenge outdated beliefs and foster a broader, more inclusive understanding of human connections.

Alternative Remedy:
A playful take on the plot and themes of *A Room with a View* can be found in *Still Life* (2021) by Sarah Winman.

CONDITION OR SITUATION:
Searching for Friendship and Acceptance

PRESCRIPTION:
Conversations with Friends (2017)
by Sally Rooney

'You underestimate your own power, so you don't have to blame yourself for treating other people badly.'

Themes of power dynamics, consent, identity and the search for meaning and connection in one's life are all explored in this book. Frances, the protagonist and narrator, is a young college student struggling to find her place in the world and to define herself. Through her interactions with Nick and Melissa, an older couple she befriends, and Bobbi, her best friend and former lover, Frances is forced to confront her own desires, needs and limitations, and to consider how these are formed by her relationships with others. The novel suggests that our identities are always in flux, and that they are shaped by the complex web of other people and power dynamics that surround us.

Rooney examines how power can be exercised and negotiated in various ways, often subtly and insidiously. The relationships between the characters are marked by a constant shifting of the dynamics, with each person seeking to assert their own desires and needs while also navigating the desires and needs of others. This is particularly evident in the relationships between Frances and Nick, and Bobbi and Melissa, where the lines between consent and coercion are often blurred.

Another significant theme of the novel is the search for meaning in life. The characters are all struggling to find their place in the world and to make sense of their lives. They are drawn to each other because they are seeking intimacy, acceptance and a sense of belonging. However, their relationships are often marked by a sense of disconnection and isolation, highlighting the difficulties of forming and maintaining meaningful links with others.

Alternative Remedy:
For a lighter exploration of the messiness of human relationships and a tale of a young woman searching for meaningful connections, try Rose Tremain's wry novel *Absolutely and Forever* (2023), set in Chelsea in the 1960s.

CONDITION OR SITUATION:
Processing a Divorce

PRESCRIPTION:
The Beauty of the Husband (2001)
by Anne Carson

*'He was like a beautiful poison, seducing me
with his words and leaving me broken.'*

Subtitled 'A Fictional Essay in 29 Tangos', *The Beauty of the Husband* is a book-length poem that studies the dissolution of a marriage using a fragmented, melodious narrative. Carson employs an unconventional method of interweaving personal reflection, references to the classics, and philosophical deliberation into her 29 'tango' verses which, as in the dance, mirror the push and pull of the relationship.

The story revolves around an unnamed female speaker as she looks back on her marriage to a charming and attractive but unfaithful man. Despite his beauty and charisma, this man is selfish, manipulative and lacking emotion, and the speaker struggles with her love for him, her deep hurt resulting from his infidelities, and the understanding of desire and loss.

The 'tangos' represent the way in which partners are drawn together by desire and then repelled by conflict, and Carson uses this to outline how, even though it is obvious to both partners that separation has become a necessity, there often remains a lingering attachment that stops couples from making a clean break.

Carson's message is that love has to be built on trust, not just on romantic desire. She teaches readers this by using the husband's beauty as a symbol of the idealized image many people have of a partner at the outset of marriage, causing them to ignore the warning signs until it becomes impossible to deny their partner's infidelities.

This work also discusses the extreme emotional toll caused by the husband's unfaithfulness and coldness, leading to psychological issues around self-doubt, dwelling in the past, and difficulties in reclaiming identity. Divorce is shown as a profoundly personal catastrophe which forces confrontation of one's vulnerabilities.

However, Carson suggests to us that divorce represents more than loss, as it can be an opportunity, even in the midst of grief, to learn more about oneself and ultimately gain empowerment.

Alternative Remedy:
Jealousy (1957) by Alain Robbe-Grillet is an experimental novel that details the psychological paranoia accompanying a marriage unravelling.

CONDITION OR SITUATION:
Toxic Relationships

PRESCRIPTION:
Women Who Love Too Much (1985)
by Robin Norwood

*'When being in love means being in
pain we are loving too much.'*

This self-help book takes a deep look into toxic relationships. It explores why some women repeatedly embark on painful, unfulfilling or destructive relationships with those who are emotionally unavailable, abusive, or unequipped to reciprocate healthy love. This tendency to be drawn to such partners is often a result of deep-rooted childhood experiences.

According to Norwood, recognizing the signs of a toxic relationship is vital, and she lists common traits of 'women who love too much', enabling the reader to identify patterns in their behaviour that they may have normalized. Once a pattern has been recognized, Norwood's exploration of early life influences or instability within family relationships can allow the reader to relate past experiences to their present choice of partners. This can provide a rationale, showing women that rather than just random attraction, they are driven by unresolved emotional needs. Norwood invites the reader to question whether their own toxic relationship is fuelled by real affection or their need to fill an emotional lacuna.

Norwood also looks at the difference between love and obsession and helps the reader to differentiate between obsessive, one-sided relationships and healthy, reciprocal ones.

Low self-esteem, emotional exhaustion, loss of self-hood, and possibly physical harm can all come from prioritizing a partner's needs over one's own, and through case studies the book advocates prioritization of one's own well-being as key to breaking free from a toxic relationship. In order to achieve this, Norwood charts steps to escape toxic dynamics such as attending therapy groups, setting boundaries and concentrating on self-love in order to regain control. Women in unhealthy relationships need to relinquish responsibility for healing their partner and focus on restoring themselves.

Women Who Love Too Much invites the reader to look at their own personal behaviours, and acts as a guide to developing healthier, more fulfilling romantic relationships.

Alternative Remedy:
Another bestselling guide to surviving toxic relationships, with a broader scope covering both sexes and same sex relationships, is *Psychopath Free* (2013) by Jackson MacKenzie.

MEDICINE CABINET ESSENTIALS:
Anna Karenina (1878)
Leo Tolstoy

Anna Karenina explores the intricacies of relationships and the mechanics of an entire culture and historical epoch – in short, it is mind-blowing. The story revolves around the lives of several aristocratic Russian families, with the central plot concerning the doomed love affair between the beautiful but flawed titular character and the raffish Count Vronsky.

However, it is much more than just a cautionary tale about the destructive nature of unchecked desire. Over the course of its 1,000 pages, Tolstoy examines the politics, religion and class of Russian society in the nineteenth century, as well as gender roles, societal expectations and family relationships. At one point the novel veers off into an in-depth analysis of land ownership and the agricultural system in Russia (Tolstoy was an avid critic and opponent of the system of serfdom) and the liberal reforms initiated in the reign of Tsar Alexander II.

A parallel narrative to Anna's infidelity concerns the struggles of Konstantin Levin. He serves as a foil to the other characters, as he grapples with existential questions and seeks a deeper connection to the world around him. Levin's story explores the tension between material comfort and spiritual fulfilment.

Anna Karenina also looks at the interplay between fate and personal agency. At the beginning of the novel Anna witnesses the accidental death of a worker at the railway station and, being superstitious, proclaims it a bad omen. The incident mirrors Anna's own fate at the end of the novel and raises questions about the extent to which individuals can control their own lives, and whether fate or circumstance plays a larger role in shaping their destinies.

Anna Karenina is a kaleidoscopic portrayal of people and society which explores universal themes of love, desire, betrayal, social class, family relationships and what it is to be human and alive.

> 'She hardly knew at times what it was she feared, and what she hoped for. Whether she feared or desired what had happened or what was going to happen and exactly what she longed for, she could not have said.'

Alternative Remedy:
Tolstoy's other grand tome *War and Peace* (1867) offers up an even more ambitious panorama of Russian society in the nineteenth century, set against the backdrop of the Napoleonic wars. Even longer than *Anna Karenina*, in *War and Peace*'s 361 chapters Tolstoy explores life, the universe and everything.

CONDITION OR SITUATION:
An Unhappy Marriage

PRESCRIPTION:
A Handful of Dust (1934)
by Evelyn Waugh

'She broke down and turning over buried her face in the pillow, in an agony of resentment and self-pity.'

This satirical novel explores the decay of moral values and the collapse of social norms among the British aristocracy in the years between the two world wars. The protagonist, Tony Last, is a member of the landed gentry who clings to outdated values, while his wife, Brenda, represents the new, modern and morally bankrupt generation.

The novel satirizes the social conventions and pretensions of the upper class, revealing the emptiness and hypocrisy beneath their polished facades. Tony's struggles to maintain his family's estate and social standing serve as a commentary on the fragility of social status and the illusion of permanence. But beneath the humour and satire, Waugh is making some pointed observations about the state of marriage in the early twentieth century. In particular, he highlights the ways in which societal expectations, class pressures and personal dissatisfaction can all combine to create a perfect storm of unhappiness in even the most seemingly perfect of unions.

A Handful of Dust warns against the dangers of moral relativism, where individuals prioritize their own desires and interests over traditional moral principles. Brenda's infidelity and the couple's subsequent divorce serve as a cautionary tale about the consequences of embracing a self-centred, hedonistic lifestyle. Waugh's novel reminds us that unhappy marriages are often the result of a deeper societal malaise – a culture that values appearances over authenticity, convenience over commitment, and personal gratification over mutual respect.

Waugh's message is one of caution, urging readers to re-examine their priorities and values in the face of a rapidly changing world. *A Handful of Dust* argues that true fulfilment and meaning can only be found by embracing a sense of purpose, morality and authenticity, rather than succumbing to the empty, materialistic pursuits of modern life – a message as pertinent today as it was in the 1920s.

Alternative Remedy:
For a much darker view of a loveless, unhappy marriage try *The Dry Heart* (1947) by Natalia Ginzburg.

CONDITION OR SITUATION:
Love in Difficult Times

PRESCRIPTION:
Love in the Time of Cholera (1985)
by Gabriel García Márquez

'Think of love as a state of grace; not the means to anything but the alpha and omega, an end in itself.'

'All you need is love,' sang The Beatles and never has this simple statement been better illustrated than by Columbian writer Gabriel García Márquez's epic novel. Set in a fictional Caribbean port city during the late nineteenth and early twentieth centuries, *Love in the Time of Cholera* recounts the love, spanning fifty years, of Florentino Ariza for Fermina Daza, a woman of a higher class than him. Against a backdrop of civil unrest, outbreaks of cholera and marked changes in society generally, the novel looks at the complexities of love in difficult times.

Due to her father's objection to the union, the young couple conduct a secret courtship until Fermina succumbs to the wishes of her father and enters into marriage with a wealthy physician. Though stable, their marriage lacks passion. Florentino is heartbroken and, despite numerous affairs, spends his whole life waiting for an opportunity for their love to be rekindled, an opportunity which arises decades later when she becomes a widow.

Throughout the novel, the author tells of the power of love and how it can be a strong and sustaining force when times are hard. Florentino's experiences of personal loss, illness and living with political instability, do not lessen his determination to one day reconnect with Fermina, and we are shown that love can become a form of insurgence against the desolation of one's social environment. *Love in the Time of Cholera* suggests to readers that love, especially when things are tough, may necessitate patience and some personal compromise, but ultimately the sacrifices are valuable and worthwhile.

After her husband's death the couple renew their relationship and Fermina has the opportunity to rediscover passion later in life. This proves to be a healing power in a time marred by disease, and their love teaches readers that even in the aftermath of hardship, love heals and renews.

Alternative Remedy:
With its blend of magic realism set against a backdrop of historical turmoil, *The House of the Spirits* (1982) by Isabel Allende is often compared to the work of Gabriel García Márquez.

CONDITION OR SITUATION:
Commitment Issues and the Fleeting Essence of Youth and Beauty

PRESCRIPTION:
The Tale of Genji (11th century)
by Murasaki Shikibu

*'How varied are the characters and
the dispositions of women!'*

We have all met or known someone who could be described as having commitment issues. It is a repetitive pattern: they fall head over heels in love, gushing wildly that they think they have finally 'found the one'. Once the initial heady rush of infatuation has faded and it's time to make a firm commitment to the relationship, suddenly they are gripped by cold fears of incompatibility, imagined or otherwise.

Often described as one of the world's first novels, or certainly the world's first psychological novel, *The Tale of Genji* was written during the eleventh century AD by a 'servant of the inner quarters' in the Japanese imperial court, the noblewoman Murasaki Shikibu. The novel centres around the exploits of the dashing Prince Genji, or more precisely his erotic adventures and dalliances with women. Genji is something of a dandy (a fair amount of admiring detail is apportioned to describing his dapper appearance and flair for fashion, especially his taste in pantaloons). However, he is no heartless, priapic seducer. He really does feel enormous love for the members of the fairer sex he encounters, at least initially, as he rattles off reams of expertly authored love poems (his favourite method of seduction).

Genji's problems stem from his inability to commit to any one of his lovers, often conducting multiple affairs simultaneously, albeit with admirable discretion. Is he gripped by a form of romantic FOMO (fear of missing out)? Is he frightened of settling for less than his grace and beauty demand? Or is he just painfully aware of the fleeting essence of youth and beauty? Certainly he is entranced by the impermanence of nature, as he conveys synaesthetic reactions to misty mountains, moonlit lakes and the changing of the seasons.

The Tale of Genji is about the enduring power of love and how, in order to truly love, we must accept the possibility of pain and loss.

Alternative Remedies:
For a less cerebral, light-hearted, if somewhat morally questionable, evocation of commitment issues in relationships try *The Ginger Man* (1955) by J. P. Donleavy. *Bridget Jones's Diary* (1996) by Helen Fielding is another humorous look at relationship problems.

CONDITION OR SITUATION:
The Perils of Forbidden Love and the Folly of Vengeance

PRESCRIPTION:
Wuthering Heights (1847)
by Emily Brontë

'Only do not leave me in this abyss, where I cannot find you!... It is unutterable! I cannot live without my life! I cannot live without my soul!'

At its core, *Wuthering Heights* is a novel about the destructive power of unchecked emotions, the dangers of toxic masculinity, and the devastating consequences of playing with fire (literally and figuratively). It's a story about the cyclical nature of trauma, the blurred lines between love and hate, and the ways in which our environments shape us into the people we become.

One recurring theme throughout the novel is people acting in bad faith and making extraordinarily poor life choices. All of the principal characters make wrong decisions that have repercussions for their lives and future happiness. Heathcliff, although badly wronged, is driven by a lust for revenge and for possession of Wuthering Heights, but this does not bring him happiness, and he dies bitter and anguished. Catherine marries Edgar Linton for profoundly the wrong reasons (money and social status) and this starts a sequence of events leading to tragedy. Similarly, Isabella and Heathcliff's marriage is also undertaken in bad faith and occasions only unhappiness and brutality.

Beneath the Gothic drama of the darker side of love, passion and revenge, Brontë also explores themes of class, identity and the social constraints of the mid-Victorian period. The novel caused quite a stir when it was first published for its challenge of established taboos and depiction of domestic and marital abuse.

Alternative Remedy:
For a different but equally withering tragedy encompassing unchained passions, cruelty, sin and lashings of Victorian hypocrisy, try Thomas Hardy's *Tess of the d'Urbervilles* (1891).

CONDITION OR SITUATION:
Rushing into Marriage

PRESCRIPTION:
Middlemarch (1871–72)
by George Eliot

'A woman dictates before marriage in order that she may have an appetite for submission afterwards.'

George Eliot's classic Victorian novel examines the lives of the inhabitants of a fictional provincial town in the midlands of England. The story follows the good people of Middlemarch as they navigate love, loss and the search for meaning in a rapidly changing world. It's a novel about the quiet struggles of ordinary people, the dangers of idealism, and the importance of empathy and understanding.

Through the eyes of Dorothea Brooke, a young woman with a heart full of ideals and a mind full of questions, Eliot explores the tensions between personal desire and social expectation, the limitations of small-town life and the challenges of finding one's place in the world. And then there's Dr Lydgate, the charming but flawed doctor who's trying to bring modern medicine to the provinces, but keeps getting tangled up in his own ego and the town's gossip mill.

One of the central themes is the role of women in society and the stifling institution of marriage, as the characters in *Middlemarch* delude themselves that they are marrying for love, but in reality are compromising themselves and conforming to a societal norm. This folly of marrying for convenience or marrying for other 'wrong' reasons is played out throughout the novel as character after character ends up in a marriage that, although not disastrous, is stultifying and unfulfilling.

So, should you have a friend or family member who you suspect may be about to tie the knot for the wrong reasons, suggest they read *Middlemarch* – at more than 800 pages it will give them plenty of time to reflect on whether they are about to make a terrible mistake.

Alternative Remedy:
Buddenbrooks (1901) by Thomas Mann has similar depth and psychological realism to *Middlemarch* and chronicles the fate of a wealthy German family over several generations.

CONDITION OR SITUATION:
Adultery or Contemplating an Affair

PRESCRIPTION:
The Good Soldier (1915)
by Ford Maddox Ford

*'Why can't people have what they want? The
things were all there to content everybody;
yet everybody has the wrong thing.'*

The temptation to have an affair can be intoxicating to some people, the chance to put some excitement and adventure back into a life that has become stale and unfulfilled. But is the grass always so much greener on the other side of the fence? *The Good Soldier* recounts the perils of adultery through the tragic tale of Edward Ashburnham and his outwardly perfect marriage that is destroyed through adultery. The novel explores the social conventions and hypocrisies of the upper class in England and Europe during the early twentieth century, revealing the emptiness and superficiality of their lives.

Through the unreliable eyes of Edward's friend John Dowell, *The Good Soldier* critiques the institution of marriage, highlighting the ways in which it can be a prison for individuals, stifling their desires and creativity. However, the book is equally adamant that adultery, no matter how enticing a prospect, can lead to devastating consequences.

Another major theme is how appearances can be deceptive and unreliable, and how people's outward lives may hide inner turmoil and conflict. The novel suggests that self-awareness and self-reflection are essential elements for personal growth and understanding, and that a lack of self-awareness can lead to decisions made in bad faith that can have shattering consequences. *The Good Soldier* is a novel that offers a nuanced and complex exploration of human relationships, identity and desire, providing its readers with a deeper understanding of the intricacies of human emotions.

Alternative Remedies:
The history of the modern novel is full of tragic tales of the heart involving adultery and deception (see also *Anna Karenina* and *Madame Bovary*), but for a slice of real anguish and hopelessness try *The End of the Affair* (1951) by Graham Greene.

MEDICINE CABINET ESSENTIALS:
Madame Bovary (1857)
by Gustave Flaubert

Everyone, from time to time, daydreams of a better life or feels that their life is just drifting along and yearns for some excitement, some adventure, something to make them feel alive. Most people are able to look upon such thoughts as wistful pipe dreams, a momentary mental distraction when taking the rubbish out or mowing the lawn or doing any other mundane chore. But it's when that yearning becomes all-consuming that problems arise. Take the case of Emma Bovary as a cautionary tale.

Madame Bovary is a novel that explores the monotony and desperation of provincial life in nineteenth-century France, and revolves around the titular character, a young woman who seeks excitement and romance in a world that seems soul-crushingly dull and unfulfilling. Emma's problem is that her head is filled with romantic ideals gleaned from reading trashy novels and she is patently unable to distinguish fantasy from reality.

Flaubert suggests that happiness is an illusion, and that people often mistake pleasure or excitement for true fulfilment. Emma's pursuit of happiness ultimately leads to her unhappiness, highlighting the elusiveness of true satisfaction.

Emma's desires, initially driven by a wish for love and connection, eventually become corrupted by her own selfishness and materialism. The novel explores how desire can consume and destroy individuals, leading to a loss of moral compass and a decline into chaos. The issue, of course, is that Emma's ideals of romantic intrigues were never going to live up to the sordid reality of actually engaging in vacuous and loveless adultery.

Madame Bovary suggests that true fulfilment and happiness can only be achieved through self-awareness, authenticity and a deep understanding of one's own values and desires. In a world where social media and consumerism often promote superficiality and conformity, the novel's message remains a powerful reminder of the importance of living an authentic and meaningful life true to the realities of things as they are, not how we may project them to be.

> *'Deep down, all the while, she waited for something to happen. Like a shipwrecked sailor, she kept casting desperate glances over the solitude of her life, seeking some white sail in the distant mists of the horizon.'*

CONDITION OR SITUATION:
Remembering the Power of Love and Friendship

PRESCRIPTION:
Captain Corelli's Mandolin (1994)
by Louis de Bernières

'Love itself is what is left over when being in love has burned away, and this is both an art and a fortunate accident.'

Set on the Greek island of Cephalonia during World War II, *Captain Corelli's Mandolin* is set on the Greek island of Cephalonia during World War II and follows the lives of the island's inhabitants, particularly Dr Iannis and his daughter Pelagia, as they face the complexities of love and the war. The novel explores the impact of war on ordinary people, showing the ways in which it disrupts lives, destroys communities and challenges moral values.

The book is a powerful exploration of love in all its forms, including romantic love, familial love and platonic love, illustrating how love can bring people together, but also how it can be tested and transformed by the challenges of war and occupation. By encouraging readers to consider the perspectives and experiences of others, particularly in the context of war, *Captain Corelli's Mandolin* explores how love, empathy and understanding can help to break down barriers and build bridges between people from different backgrounds.

The novel also offers up a portrayal of the complexities of human nature by showing the ways in which people can be both good and bad, brave and cowardly, selfless and selfish. Another theme is the importance of forgiveness and reconciliation, particularly in the aftermath of conflict and trauma, and the book demonstrates how these processes can help to heal wounds and rebuild relationships. Ultimately, though, de Bernières' message is about the importance of love and relationships in giving our lives meaning and purpose, and how these connections can help us to survive even the most challenging circumstances.

Alternative Remedy:
For an alternative dose of tales of love and loss set on a Greek island during the war try *The Island* (2005) by Victoria Hislop, which uses Spinalonga – a former leper colony – as its backdrop.

CONDITION OR SITUATION:
Obsessive Love

PRESCRIPTION:
Enduring Love (1997)
by Ian McEwan

'De Clérambault's syndrome was a dark, distorting mirror that reflected and parodied a brighter world of lovers whose reckless abandon to their cause was sane.'

In *Enduring Love*, Ian McEwan masterfully explores several complex and interconnected themes that probe the human condition. One of the primary concerns of the novel is the nature of love and obsession. Through the character of Jed Parry, McEwan examines the darker aspects of love, revealing how it can quickly tip into an all-consuming and destructive force. Jed has de Clérambault's syndrome (erotomania), a condition that makes him obsess over someone he fantasizes is in love with him. In contrast, the relationship between Joe Rose and his partner Clarissa embodies a more rational and enduring form of love, highlighting the difference between passion and reason.

The novel also explores the theme of science versus emotion, as embodied by Joe's rational, scientific worldview and Jed's fervent, emotional religiosity. McEwan raises important questions about the limitations of scientific knowledge and the role of emotion in human experience, suggesting that a solely rational approach to life can be inadequate and even dangerous. In addition, the novel touches on the power of narrative and storytelling. Through Joe's attempts to make sense of the events that unfold, McEwan comments on the ways in which we construct narratives to impose order on our lives, and the ways in which these narratives can both reveal and conceal the truth.

Furthermore, *Enduring Love* is a novel about the fragility of human relationships and the unpredictability of human behaviour. The catastrophic event that opens the novel – a hot air balloon accident – serves as a catalyst for the exploration of these themes, highlighting the ways in which chance and circumstance can disrupt even the most seemingly stable lives.

Alternative Remedy:
Another work that tackles pathological and obsessive love is John Fowles' novel *The Collector* (1963).

CONDITION OR SITUATION:
Dealing with the Past and the Passage of Time

PRESCRIPTION:
The Museum of Innocence (2008)
by Orhan Pamuk

'In poetically well-built museums, formed from the heart's compulsions, we are consoled not by finding in them old objects that we love, but by losing all sense of Time.'

This novel by Turkish Nobel Prize-winner Orhan Pamuk explores themes of love, obsession, memory and the passage of time. Set in Istanbul in the 1970s and 1980s, the narrative follows Kemal, a wealthy man who becomes infatuated with his distant relative Füsun, a lowly shop assistant. Despite being engaged to another woman, Kemal seduces Füsun and embarks upon a brief but torrid love affair. It is only when Füsun suddenly disappears that Kemal realizes the depth of his feelings for her and he sinks into a state of melancholic yearning and despair.

When Kemal finally meets Füsun again she is married, but still living with her parents, and he takes to visiting her every week for dinner. Kemal's obsession with Füsun leads him to collect objects associated with her and their love, which he later displays in a museum dedicated to their relationship.

The novel delves into the nature of obsessive love and how it can consume an individual's life. Kemal's fixation on Füsun becomes a central force driving his actions and decisions. A key theme is the power of memory and mournful nostalgia. Pamuk uses the Turkish term *hüzün* – which roughly translates as melancholy but also denotes a spiritual state of mind caused by a place of loss and grief. The objects Kemal collects serve as tangible memories of his time with Füsun, highlighting how people use physical items to hold onto the past, preserve memories and navigate their emotional landscapes.

The novel also examines the social and cultural changes in Istanbul during the late twentieth century, particularly focusing on class differences, the impact of Westernization and the status of women in Turkish society. The passage of time and the inevitability of loss are recurring motifs. Kemal's museum becomes a way to immortalize his love and resist the erasure of time.

Alternative Remedy:
For another dose of Turkish *hüzün* and the pain of missed opportunities and lost love try *Madonna in a Fur Coat* (1943) by Sabahattin Ali.

CONDITION OR SITUATION:
Living in the Past/Revisiting Past Love

PRESCRIPTION:
The Great Gatsby (1925)
by F. Scott Fitzgerald

'There must have been moments even that afternoon when Daisy tumbled short of his dreams – not through her own fault but because of the colossal vitality of his illusion.'

Imagine the ultimate house party – lavish decor, fancy cars and champagne toasts. But, beneath the glittering surface, it's a bubbling cauldron of secrets, scandals and unrequited love. F. Scott Fitzgerald's classic novel is like a juicy gossip column, exposing the dark underbelly of the American Dream. It's a tale of wealth and excess in the Roaring Twenties, an era of unabashed decadence.

The story of Gatsby's meteoric rise and downfall is recounted by Nick Carraway, an observer of the fashionable society he seeks to inhabit. Carraway describes the characters around him, their relationships, motivations, hypocrisies and deceits. It is with barely concealed glee that the narrator recounts the rumours that swirl around the enigmatic Gatsby and where his fabulous wealth has come from.

Against the decadent backdrop, Fitzgerald explores the tension between 'old money' and 'new money'. This conflict is neatly represented by the residential locations in the book. Gatsby and Carraway – the aspirational *nouveau riche* – live at West Egg. On the other hand, East Egg is the home of those who have inherited their wealth, such as Gatsby's lost first love Daisy Buchanan and her husband Tom. Despite his abundant riches, Gatsby's wealth can't turn back time and make Daisy marry him, the one thing he truly craves. Nor can his wealth buy him a place at the 'old money' dinner table (although quite why he would want to dine with shallow, insufferable snobs and hypocrites is anyone's guess).

Gatsby's rags-to-riches story and fall from grace is the ultimate symbol of the hollowness of the American Dream, but it's also a cautionary tale about the corrupting influence of wealth and the elusiveness of true happiness. The book also warns against trying to recreate the fleeting happiness or ardour from the past, and shows how elusive and forever out of reach that will ultimately be.

Alternative Remedy:
The Chosen and the Beautiful (2021) by Nghi Vo retells the story of Gatsby from the point of view of Jordan Baker, Nick Carraway's on/off love interest (and the reason for Jordan's perceived diffidence in the original novel is startlingly revealed).

CONDITION OR SITUATION:
Learning Lessons from the Past and Valuing Friendship

PRESCRIPTION:
My Ántonia (1918)
by Willa Cather

*'Whatever we had missed, we possessed together
the precious, the incommunicable past.'*

Maybe it's an age thing, but the past often seems a place of comfort, especially when thinking about past friendships. This is particularly so for connections that have been broken through no accident or injury but just by the inexorable passing of time. One novel that can tell us a lot about the value of past friendships is Willa Cather's *My Ántonia*. The story revolves around the complex and deeply emotional relationship between Jim Burden, a young boy from the East Coast of the USA, and Ántonia Shimerda, a Czech immigrant girl, as they grow up together on the Nebraska frontier.

The themes of the immigrant experience, the American frontier and friendship are deeply interconnected in Cather's novel. The struggles faced by Ántonia and her family are mirrored in the broader narrative of life on the land at the frontier, illustrating the complex and often fraught nature of American identity.

Through Jim's narrative, which relies heavily on the use of flashbacks, Cather explores the complexities of memory and nostalgia, revealing how the past is filtered through the lens of the present. The novel shows how our understanding of the past is often fragmented and subjective, influenced by personal experiences, cultural background and social context.

My Ántonia also foregrounds the transformative power of friendship, demonstrating how bonds can form between people from different backgrounds and places. Through the story of Jim and Ántonia, Cather illustrates the importance of empathy, understanding and forging authentic human connections in breaking down social and cultural barriers.

Alternative Remedy:
For another novel that explores the legacy of the past and old relationships through use of flashbacks, both literally and metaphorically, try *Kindred* (1979) by Octavia E. Butler – a proto-science fiction novel that transports an African-American woman from 1980 back to a slave plantation in early nineteenth-century Maryland.

CONDITION OR SITUATION:
Being Haunted by the Past

PRESCRIPTION:
The Go-Between (1953)
by L. P. Hartley

*'The past is a foreign country;
they do things differently there.'*

The above quote is the immortal first line of *The Go-Between*, a novel prescribed for anyone haunted by past events and regrets, and seeking catharsis. The story follows Leo Colston, a young boy who spends a summer at a wealthy friend's country estate, where he becomes embroiled in a complicated web of adult relationships and desires. At the centre of this intrigue is the illicit affair between Marian, the sister of Leo's friend and daughter of the lord of the manor, and a local working-class farmer. The innocent and naïve Leo becomes involved in the affair by acting as the titular 'go-between' carrying messages between the two lovers. As Leo wades through the treacherous waters of adolescence, he finds himself caught between his loyalty to his friend and his growing awareness of the secrets and lies that surround him.

One of the main themes of the novel is the corrupting influence of nostalgia. Hartley's prose is infused with a sense of wistfulness and longing as Leo looks back on his childhood with a mix of fondness and regret. However, this nostalgia is also tinged with a sense of sadness and loss, as Leo realizes that the past is irretrievable, and that the memories he holds dear are ultimately bittersweet.

The novel also explores social class and the rigid social hierarchies of the time. The wealthy family at the centre of the novel are trapped in a world of their own making, with its own set of strict rules and conventions. In contrast, the socially awkward Leo with his regional accent is very much an outsider, as is the farmer Ted Burgess. They both struggle to navigate the complexities of the upper-class world into which they have been thrust.

Although haunted by the past and the tragic events he had unwittingly become the antagonist of, Leo is offered a partial redemption at the end of the novel, suggesting that rather than burying our memories of trauma, if we can find the strength to confront them we can find a pathway towards moving on.

Alternative Remedy:
For other novels describing illicit love affairs between the classes but with a much more raunchy punch, try *Lady Chatterley's Lover* (1928) by D. H. Lawrence.

CONDITION OR SITUATION:
Love Triangles

PRESCRIPTION:
Les Liaisons Dangereuses (1782)
by Pierre Choderlos de Laclos

'I am astonished at the pleasure one feels at doing good. And I should be tempted to believe that those whom we call virtuous do not have so much merit as we are led to believe.'

An epistolary novel, *Les Liaisons Dangereuses* is a deliciously wicked tale of seduction, manipulation and the moral decay prevalent in the eighteenth-century French aristocracy.

At its core, the novel is a scathing critique of the aristocracy's moral bankruptcy, where the pursuit of pleasure and power has become the only game in town. The story follows the exploits of the Vicomte de Valmont and the Marquise de Merteuil, two former lovers turned rival manipulators, who engage in a series of intricate and ruthless games of seduction, using their charm, beauty and cunning to destroy the reputations and lives of those around them.

Through their letters, Laclos masterfully exposes the hypocrisy and corruption of the aristocracy, revealing a world where adultery is not only tolerated but also encouraged, as long as it's done with style and discretion. The Vicomte and the Marquise are the embodiment of this moral decay, using their intelligence and wit to justify their actions and manipulate others into doing their bidding.

For anyone entangled in a love triangle or hopelessly addicted to a cycle of dangerous and exciting intrigue (spoiler alert), nobody ends up happy in this novel and most characters, despite their deceit, pretty much end up ruined by their own lust, self-serving arrogance, ego and conceit.

Alternative Remedy:
Historical romances are a popular sub-genre of romantic fiction and if bodice-bursting erotic intrigues are your thing, try *Noble Satyr* (2023) by Lucinda Brant – the first in a series of novels about the decadent French aristocracy in the eighteenth century.

2

Remedies for the Soul and Spirit

CONDITION OR SITUATION:
Seeking Redemption

PRESCRIPTION:
The Power and the Glory (1940)
by Graham Greene

'That was another mystery: it sometimes seemed to him that venial sins – impatience, an unimportant lie, pride, a neglected opportunity – cut off from grace more completely than the worst sins of all.'

It is not uncommon for people of all religions to question their faith at some point in their lives; many biblical characters have found themselves questioning their god, and even Jesus himself spent forty days and forty nights trying to understand it all. *The Power and the Glory* explores a range of complex and deeply philosophical themes that probe the nature of faith, morality and human existence. One of the primary concerns of the novel is the tension between faith and doubt, the very space where much theological discourse resides, and this tension is embodied by the 'whisky priest', a term Greene coined that is now used to describe a Catholic priest who is agonized by his failure to live up to the expected standards. The flawed and often despairing whisky priest is struggling to maintain his faith in a world that seems to have abandoned God.

The novel also looks at redemption and the possibility of personal transformation. Despite his many mistakes, the whisky priest is a deeply humane and relatable character who is capable of great love, compassion and sacrifice. Greene suggests that redemption is always possible, even for those who have failed or fallen, and that it is never too late to seek forgiveness, make amends and do what is right.

Through the priest's journey, Greene raises profound questions about the nature of faith, the role of the Church, and the human condition, highlighting the difficulties of living a life of spiritual integrity in a world that is often hostile to it.

Alternative Remedies:

For other novels depicting characters grappling with the tension between faith and doubt just about any other novel by Graham Greene contains tormented Catholics, particularly *The Heart of the Matter* (1948) and *The End of the Affair* (1951). For a lighter, satirical look at religious wrangling try *The Ball and the Cross* (1909) by G. K. Chesterton.

CONDITION OR SITUATION:
Questioning One's Faith/Sexuality

PRESCRIPTION:
Go Tell It on the Mountain (1953)
by James Baldwin

*'You might think of it as a curse, but I think of
it as a blessing – every trial is a lesson.'*

Questioning one's faith and wondering where one's identities truly align are common rites-of-passage issues for young people, perhaps even more so for those growing up in communities where a strict church plays a pivotal part in people's lives. *Go Tell It on the Mountain*, a semi-autobiographical novel, addresses these problems within the wider African–American experience. Set in the 1930s in Harlem, New York, the novel follows the story of John Grimes, a fourteen-year-old boy struggling to find his place within his family, community and the world.

The novel critiques the rigid and oppressive nature of the Christian church, which is portrayed as a source of both comfort and suffocation for the characters. Baldwin explores the ways in which religion can be used to control and manipulate individuals, particularly within the context of racism and oppression, by illuminating the tensions between John's desire for autonomy and his need for belonging within his family and community. Through John's struggles, Baldwin highlights the challenges of navigating multiple identities, including racial, religious, cultural and sexual.

Go Tell It on the Mountain touches on the theme of same-sex desire, which was a taboo subject at the time of the novel's publication. By describing John's conflict with his own desires, Baldwin explores the complexities of human sexuality and the ways in which societal norms can stifle individual expression. Through John's questioning of his faith and his own identity and desires, readers can learn about the importance of self-expression and authenticity. The message of the novel is the need for individuals to be true to themselves, even in the face of societal pressure and expectation.

Alternative Remedy:
Invisible Man (1952) by Ralph Ellison, a contemporary of James Baldwin, covers similar themes of searching for identity, facing oppression and conflict, and questioning one's place in the world.

CONDITION OR SITUATION:
Being in Need of Spiritual Sustenance

PRESCRIPTION:
Siddhartha (1922)
by Hermann Hesse

'Within Siddhartha there slowly grew and ripened the knowledge of what wisdom really was ... It was nothing but a preparation of the soul, a capacity, a secret art of thinking, feeling and breathing thoughts of unity at every moment of life.'

Many people increasingly feel disconnected from the world around them, bereft of spiritual sustenance that could provide strength and direction like a guiding light in the gloom. *Siddhartha* explores the search for meaning and purpose in life, seeking to provide the reader with a broad understanding of how to achieve spiritual growth. Set in ancient India, the novel traces the life of Siddhartha, a young Indian prince, as he travels on a journey of self-discovery and spiritual exploration, delving into the complexities of Buddhism and Hinduism to find spiritual fulfilment.

Siddhartha learns the importance of letting go of self-worth and attachment to material things, and embarking upon the unknown. Meditation and mindfulness are also explored within the novel, chronicling the importance of Siddhartha's experience of developing and cultivating a sense of inner peace and awareness. An important part of this process is to learn to live in the present moment, embrace the beauty and wonder of the present moment and relinquish attachment to the past along with expectations of the future.

Hesse provides insight into the concept of non-duality, a philosophical tradition within Hinduism and a principle employed by various spiritual practices. It is the idea that the perception of individual selves, objects and experiences is an illusion. Siddhartha's discoveries within the world around him remind us of the importance of banishing dualities in order to find ultimate peace.

By following his journey of discovery, *Siddhartha* presents the reader with an influential and nuanced study of spirituality, along with a deeper understanding of the themes of spiritual exploration, inner transformation and the interconnectedness of all things. It's the perfect remedy for those searching for meaning and purpose in life.

Alternative Remedy:
For a heart-warming modern fable of a journey to self-realization which explores freedom and individuality, try *The Hen Who Dreamed She Could Fly* (2000) by Korean writer Sun-Mi Hwang.

CONDITION OR SITUATION:
Feeling Lost in the World

PRESCRIPTION:
The Quest (1911)
by Frederik van Eeden

*'He did not yet know that it is often better to let
beautiful conceptions rest, for the reason that, upon
earth, consummated works are sometimes really
less fine and striking than incomplete ones.'*

It is common at certain times in life to feel oneself drifting along, lost and directionless. Many of the works discussed in *100 Books to Live By* are concerned with the search for meaning in life, with protagonists undergoing a journey either redemptive or enlightening, and the central character of Frederik van Eeden's novel is no exception. *The Quest* is both a fantasy and a philosophical and psychological novel that follows the journey of a young man named Little Johannes as he searches for purpose in his life. The story is a symbolic and introspective exploration of the human condition, delving into themes of spirituality, morality and the search for truth.

Little Johannes lives in an old house surrounded by a sumptuous garden that he has transformed in his mind into a magical and enchanted micro-universe. As Johannes explores his environment, his vivid imagination allows him to think of his surroundings as a grand realm. One evening, he encounters Windekind, a vivid manifestation of nature, who takes him on marvellous adventures filled with strange and profound discoveries.

The novel explores various spiritual and philosophical traditions including Christianity, Buddhism and mysticism, as Johannes seeks to understand the nature of existence and his place in the world. Through Johannes' journey, van Eeden argues that being lost is a natural and necessary part of the human experience, and that it can be a catalyst for growth and transformation.

The Quest shows that uncertainty and doubt can be an essential part of the journey towards self-discovery and understanding, and that introspection and self-reflection can be valuable tools in facing the challenges of life and how to find one's way.

Alternative Remedy:
Another novel that masterfully blends philosophical investigation with wild flights of fantasy and fairy tale is *Sophie's World* (1991) by Norwegian author Jostein Gaarder.

MEDICINE CABINET ESSENTIALS:
I Know Why the Caged Bird Sings (1969)
by Maya Angelou

Maya Angelou's *I Know Why the Caged Bird Sings* is an autobiographical novel published in 1969. The first in a series of seven autobiographies, it tells the story of Maya's childhood and adolescence growing up as a black girl in the segregated South of the United States. The novel shows Maya's journey towards self-discovery and identity as she manages her own sense of self-worth, traversing the complexities of being in a society that devalues her existence.

Maya's story is an important illustration of the value of family and community. Her relationships with her brother, mother and grandmother are particularly significant, and they provide her with a sense of belonging and support. The memoir is also a celebration of the power of literature and education to transform lives. Maya finds solace and inspiration in the works of authors such as Shakespeare and Dickens, and she recognizes the importance of education in empowering herself and her community, encouraging us to also foster a love of literature and learning.

Angelou encourages readers to consider the experiences of others, particularly those who have been marginalized or oppressed. The book promotes empathy and understanding, and it challenges readers to think critically about the social and cultural norms that shape our lives.

Maya's journey is also a powerful reminder of the importance of self-care and self-love. She inspires readers to prioritize their own well-being and to cultivate a positive sense of self-worth.

> *'The caged bird sings with a fearful trill,*
> *of things unknown, but longed for still,*
> *and his tune is heard on the distant hill,*
> *for the caged bird sings of freedom.'*

CONDITION OR SITUATION:
Contemplating the Fragility of Existence

PRESCRIPTION:
The Unbearable Lightness of Being (1984)
by Milan Kundera

'The heavier the burden, the closer our lives come to the earth, the more real and truthful they become.'

Imagine a novel that's like an existential Czech soap opera, but with more sex, less conflict, and a healthy dose of philosophical angst. That is pretty much the sum of *The Unbearable Lightness of Being* by Milan Kundera.

The novel follows the lives of four main characters: at the centre is Tomáš, a charming but commitment-phobic surgeon – the Czech equivalent of a 1960s playboy who can undress women by raising an eyebrow (eat your heart out, James Bond); Tereza is Tomáš' beautiful and brooding wife who is the human equivalent of a rainy Sunday afternoon; Sabina, Tomáš' free-spirited mistress, is a hippie version of a femme fatale, and finally there is Franz, a Swiss academic who is dependable if dull, and moons over Sabina like a besotted puppy dog.

As these characters navigate love, sex and relationships in 1960s Prague, they must also contend with the crushing weight of existential dread, the absurdity of life under communism, and the search for purpose in a seemingly meaningless world.

The novel attempts a philosophical inversion of the concept of 'eternal return', a theory that explores the notion that time repeats itself in an infinite (eternal) loop. The theory dates from the Stoic philosophers of Ancient Greece, but was revived and explored in the nineteenth century through the writings of Friedrich Wilhelm Nietzsche. Kundera rejected the eternal return in favour of the view that we only live once, so our lives are fleeting and meaningless – they weigh lightly upon the universe. This is the burden that is 'the unbearable lightness of being'.

Alternative Remedies:
Modernist/existential novels were all the rage in European fiction in the first half of the twentieth century and several notable examples are examined in later sections of this book (see *Hunger*, *The Outsider* and *The Trial*). But for a neat extrapolation of the meaninglessness of life try *Nausea* (1938) by 'Mr Existentialism' himself, Jean-Paul Sartre.

CONDITION OR SITUATION:
Feeling Lost and Uncertain

PRESCRIPTION:
I May Be Wrong (2022)
by Björn Natthiko Lindeblad

'Human life is short. When we truly understand that, when we stop taking each other and what we have for granted, then we move through our own lives differently.'

Feelings of being lost and uncertain are common, especially in dark times or when someone reaches middle age and it seems like all the fun and excitement of life has passed. *I May Be Wrong* is a memoir by a former Swedish businessman who became a Buddhist forest monk (one who lives in an isolated woodland monastery) in Thailand for seventeen years before returning to secular life. The book recounts Lindeblad's extraordinary journey of self-discovery, spiritual exploration and eventual confrontation with terminal illness. The title reflects a key philosophy Lindeblad adopted during his monastic life: the willingness to admit 'I may be wrong,' an admission that fosters humility and openness to growth.

During his years as a monk, Lindeblad learns the practice of mindfulness – being fully present in the moment without judgement. For readers feeling lost, this offers a tool to anchor themselves amid chaos. Lindeblad suggests that instead of obsessing over finding the 'right' path, one can find peace by focusing on the here and now, reducing the anxiety of an uncertain future.

Lindeblad's decision to leave a conventional, 'successful' life for the unknown of monastic living illustrates that feeling lost can be a catalyst for transformation. He teaches that uncertainty is not a failure but an opportunity to explore deeper truths about oneself. By admitting 'I may be wrong,' he encourages readers to let go of rigid beliefs or societal expectations and remain open to new perspectives, even when the future is unclear.

I May Be Wrong teaches that feeling lost and uncertain is an inevitable part of life's journey, but it doesn't have to be a dead end. Lindeblad's story encourages readers to view these emotions as invitations to slow down, reflect and cultivate resilience through humility, mindfulness and acceptance. His life, marked by radical choices and profound challenges, serves as a reminder that peace can sometimes be found not in having all the answers, but in learning to live gracefully with the questions.

Alternative Remedy:
Well, perhaps there is only one alternative remedy. That's to read the big cheese himself and dive into *The Four Noble Truths* (1997) by the 14th Dalai Lama.

CONDITION OR SITUATION:
Crises of Faith

PRESCRIPTION:
The Name of the Rose (1980)
by Umberto Eco

'True learning must not be content with ideas, which are, in fact, signs, but must discover things in their individual truth.'

Umberto Eco's *The Name of the Rose* is a historical mystery novel. The action takes place in 1327, in a Benedictine abbey in northern Italy, where a Franciscan friar named William of Baskerville and his young apprentice, Adso of Melk, arrive to attend a theological disputation. However, their visit soon turns into a murder investigation as a series of mysterious deaths occur in the abbey.

One of the main themes of the novel is the tension between the pursuit of knowledge and the fear of knowledge. The power of knowledge is symbolized by the abbey's library, which contains ancient and forbidden texts. This is contrasted with the dangers of ignorance and the suppression of truth, represented by the murders and the subsequent cover-up. Eco also highlights the conflict between faith and reason as embodied by the characters of William, a rational and sceptical investigator, and the abbey's monks, who are driven by dogma and superstition. The novel suggests that faith and reason are not mutually exclusive, but rather complementary aspects of human understanding.

The abbey is portrayed as a microcosm of the corrupt and decadent society of the time. The abbey's leaders, who are more concerned with maintaining their power and privilege than with seeking truth and justice, are willing to go to great lengths to suppress dissent and keep their grip on authority.

Umberto Eco was a renowned academic in the field of semiotics, the science of signs and symbols, and *The Name of the Rose* is a celebration of the art of interpretation and the importance of understanding the signs and symbols that surround us. William's expertise in semiotics and his ability to read the signs of the abbey's architecture, art and literature are crucial to solving the mystery.

The Name of the Rose suggests that human understanding is fragile and provisional, and that our perceptions of reality are always subject to revision and reinterpretation.

Alternative Remedy:
For another epic novel rich in philosophical and theological disputation try *The Discovery of Heaven* (1992) by Dutch author Harry Mulisch.

CONDITION OR SITUATION:
Starting the Grieving Process

PRESCRIPTION:
The White Book (2016)
by Han Kang

'I wanted to show you clean things. Before brutality, sadness, despair, filth, pain, clean things that were only for you, clean things above all ... Again and again I peered into your eyes, as though searching for form in a deep, black mirror.'

It is often said that people suffering a bereavement struggle to know how to grieve, at least at first. It can feel as if seeking to move on is somehow a betrayal of the person who has been lost. There is also, perhaps, a pressure – real or imaginary – to be strong for the sake of other family members and friends, which can stifle the very personal and individual need to grieve. It can sometimes help to hear how someone else has approached the grieving process, perhaps by joining a bereavement group or through reading others' experiences of the process.

Nobel Prize-winning Korean writer Han Kang's novelized memoir *The White Book* is a moving autobiographical account of trying to come to terms with grief and loss. The writer is on a retreat in Warsaw, Poland and as she moves through the city she observes the scars and traces of World War II. This brings to mind the wounds of trauma she has experienced, both personal and political. Han recalls her younger baby sister, who died two hours after birth, and tries to recreate her mentally through a list of white objects, either overtly or obliquely related to her sister's short life. The novel is written in a fragmentary, shimmering style which lends it a dream-like quality that gradually develops into a deeply moving treatise on grief, memory and transcendence, and the nature of loss.

Alternative Remedies:

A more straightforward memoir about beginning the grieving process is *The Year of Magical Thinking* (2005) by Joan Didion, which details the first year following the death of her husband. *The Beginner's Goodbye* (2012) by Anne Tyler is a sad yet uplifting and insightful novel about a widower dealing with the sudden death of his wife in a freak accident.

CONDITION OR SITUATION:
The Sudden Death of a Loved One

PRESCRIPTION:
After You'd Gone (2000)
by Maggie O'Farrell

*'Why isn't life better designed so it warns you
when terrible things are about to happen?'*

The novel *After You'd Gone* revolves around the central character of Alice Raikes, a young woman who, after a tragic accident, ends up in a coma. As she hovers between life and death, the narrative explores her past, her relationships and the events that led up to the accident. The novel tackles the aftermath of traumatic events and the processes of grief and recovery, looking at how these experiences can shape us and the ways in which we cope with pain and loss.

The book also delves into the complexities of family connections, examining the bonds between mothers, daughters, sisters and partners. *After You'd Gone* highlights the ways in which our relationships and the secrets we keep from one another also shape us and looks at the consequences of unspoken secrets and unresolved conflicts. The book emphasizes the need for open and honest communication.

The novel also demonstrates how our memories, both individual and collective, affect our understanding of ourselves and our place in the world. At the same time, it points to the subjective nature of memories and the ways in which our recollections can be influenced by our emotions, biases and experiences.

After You'd Gone encourages readers to consider the complexities of human experience and the importance of empathy and understanding in our relationships with others. Despite the traumatic events that unfold, the book ultimately offers a message of hope and resilience, showing how people can find ways to heal, recover and move forward in the face of adversity.

Alternative Remedy:
Finding ways to articulate grief to young people can be incredibly challenging, especially after the sudden death of a family member. Michael Rosen's *Sad Book* (2004), written in response to the death of his own son, is a moving, simple and sincere evocation of complex emotional pain to help children and parents alike.

MEDICINE CABINET ESSENTIALS:
What We Talk About When We Talk About Love (1981)
by Raymond Carver

It isn't just novels or memoirs that can teach us important life lessons that can inspire us or heal our predicaments with their insights. A good short story can reveal much about the world around us by catching moments in microcosm, snapshots of lives undergoing transitions or discovering sudden flashes of truth.

What We Talk About When We Talk About Love is a collection of seventeen short stories. Each is a brief vignette or window into the lives of ordinary Americans, exploring their loneliness or sense of disconnection. Unhappy or unfulfilling relationships loom large over these stories, as do communication problems between people grappling to articulate the suffering of their souls: a young couple mourning the tragic death of their young son find themselves the prey of a vindictive baker who had made a cake for the dead child's birthday; four friends find the corpse of a young woman while on a fishing trip but don't report it because it would ruin their vacation; a dysfunctional young couple embark on a macabre tug of war over their own baby. Story after story is inhabited by people bent out of shape

by life, chewed up and spat out again. Carver's characters have flaws and delusions, lost dreams and fading ambitions for what their lives could or should have been, all beautifully evoked in brittle, emotively brutal prose.

Reading Carver stories reminds readers of the struggles of everyday life that most people go through and that listening to other people's pain and suffering fosters compassion and solidarity, easing their burden and strife:

> *'Then he began to talk. They listened carefully. Although they were tired and in anguish, they listened to what the baker had to say. They listened, nodded when the baker began to speak of loneliness, and of the sense of doubt and limitation that had come to him in his middle years. He told them what it was like to be childless all these years. To repeat the days with the ovens endlessly full and endlessly empty.'*

CONDITION OR SITUATION:
Needing to Build Resilience

PRESCRIPTION:
Life of Pi (2001)
by Yann Martel

'Something in me did not want to give up on life, was unwilling to let go, wanted to fight to the very end. Where that part of me got the heart, I don't know.'

Yann Martel's 2001 *Life of Pi* is both an adventure and a philosophical story about an Indian sixteen-year-old named Piscine Molitor Patel, known as Pi, and his recounting of the remarkable journey he was forced to make. Pi was raised in both a multi-religious and multicultural society, and the novel draws upon Hinduism, Christianity and Islam. It is a mystical tale as well as one of survival and resilience.

Pi's family, who own a zoo in India, decide to emigrate to Canada, taking their animals along with them on a cargo ship. The ship disastrously sinks in the Pacific Ocean, with the only survivors being Pi, a wounded zebra, a hyena, an orangutan and a Bengal tiger. Pi tells of his distressing 227-day ordeal at sea in a lifeboat with his fellow survivors and of the resourceful techniques he employs to keep himself alive against the odds.

Eventually, only Pi and the tiger are left, and Pi manages to keep them both alive by fishing for food while at the same time experiencing extreme terror of the powerful creature. Pi overcomes his fear by not succumbing to panic and instead realizing that they both need each other, and that he has to train the tiger. This helps guide us to the understanding and importance of using the mind to re-evaluate life's difficulties in order to find solutions even in what appear to be hopeless situations.

Pi's relationship with the tiger becomes a lifeline for him as caring for the animal gives him a sense of responsibility, helps him cope with the isolation, and gives him a reason to keep going. The acts of repeatedly catching a fish or collecting rainwater emphasize to the reader that persistence in small, mundane, though crucial tasks builds strength.

Life of Pi demonstrates the resilience that human beings are capable of even under the most profound hardships, by adopting mental, emotional and spiritual strategies in order to stay alive as well as adapt to their circumstances.

Alternative Remedy:
Another book that examines undertaking a spiritual journey with a feline is Genki Kawamura's *If Cats Disappeared from the World* (2012).

CONDITION OR SITUATION:
Questioning the Power of the Human Spirit

PRESCRIPTION:
The Hunger Angel (2009)
by Herta Müller

'To combat death you don't need much of a life, just one that isn't finished yet.'

Sometimes we need reminding just how remarkable and resilient people can be when faced with indescribable hardship. We might bemoan our lot, or feel hard done by, but we can draw inspiration and strength from novels that provide stirring examples of the triumph of the human spirit.

The Hunger Angel is set in a Soviet labour camp in the 1950s, where the protagonist, Leo Auberg, is imprisoned for five years. The novel follows Leo's journey as he confronts the harsh conditions of the labour camp, where he is forced to work in a coal mine and struggle to survive on meagre rations. Despite the brutal conditions, Leo finds ways to maintain his dignity and humanity, and to hold on to his memories of his past life.

Müller's writing is revered for its lyrical and poetic style, and *The Hunger Angel* is no exception. The novel is written in a beautiful, evocative prose that captures the brutality of the labour camp and the inner lives of the characters. The novel is rich in symbolism and metaphor, with objects, events and characters imbued with layers of meaning or representing abstract ideas and concepts. Through her literary devices, Müller foregrounds the importance of language and culture in shaping our experiences and the ways in which they can be used as tools of resistance and survival. Leo's story shows us that even in the most extreme conditions, individuals can find ways to create and express themselves and to maintain a sense of purpose and meaning.

The Hunger Angel is a powerful testament to the triumph of the human spirit and a reminder that, even in the darkest of times, there is always hope and a way to survive. The book is a profound celebration of the human capacity for resilience, creativity and endurance.

Alternative Remedies:

There are many books that inspire with their tales of resilience in the face of adversity. See, for example, *One Day in the Life of Ivan Denisovich*. But few books have to overcome extreme adversity to be written at all. *The Diving Bell and the Butterfly* (1997) is one such. This is a memoir by French journalist Jean-Dominique Bauby, who was paralysed after a stroke and unable to communicate except by blinking his left eye in different patterns to spell out words.

CONDITION OR SITUATION:
Wistfulness

PRESCRIPTION:
Life Begins on Friday (2009)
by Ioana Pârvulescu

'For a few years before 1900 the days were capacious. The people thrummed like telegraph wires. They were optimistic and believed, like never before and never thereafter, in the power of science, in progress and the future.'

Have you ever yearned for some previous phase of your life? Such nostalgia might be accompanied by a curious melancholy for that earlier world you lived in, which you are now seeing through rose-tinted lenses. In *Life Begins on Friday* Romanian writer Ioana Pârvulescu explores a range of themes relating to history and the past. One of the primary concerns of the novel is the nature of identity and how it is shaped by cultural, social and historical contexts. Through the tale of the protagonist, time traveller Dan Kretzu, Pârvulescu raises questions about the ways in which our sense of self is influenced by the world around us, and how we navigate the complexities of identity in a rapidly changing world.

The novel also explores the theme of time and its relationship to human experience. It is structured around a series of events that unfold in the city of Bucharest over the last two weeks of the year 1897. Through this structure, Pârvulescu highlights the ways in which our experiences of time are subjective and relative, and how our perceptions of the past, present and future are shaped by our individual perspectives.

Another major theme of the novel is the power of storytelling and the role of narrative in forming our view of the world. Dan Kretzu is a writer, and the novel is full of references to literature, history and mythology. Through these references, Pârvulescu explores the ways in which stories can both reflect and shape our understanding of reality, and how they can be used to create new meanings and possibilities.

Ultimately, *Life Begins on Friday* is a novel about the search for meaning and connection in a chaotic and often confusing world. Through Kretzu's journey back through time, Pârvulescu raises questions about the nature of reality, the human condition and the search for transcendence and purpose. The novel is a deeply philosophical and introspective work that challenges readers to think critically about the world around them and their place within it.

Alternative Remedy:
Another novel that explores the texture of time and memory is *Ada, or Ardor: A Family Chronicle* (1969) by Vladimir Nabokov.

MEDICINE CABINET ESSENTIALS:
Meditations (167 AD)
by Marcus Aurelius

Imagine, if you will, being on a boat that has a library below deck. (The ill-fated RMS *Titanic* had two libraries for first- and second-class passengers – the presumption being perhaps that third-class or steerage passengers were illiterate.) In the boat's library are all of the titles mentioned here in this book, plus a few more besides. The boat hits an iceberg and is sinking fast and, knowing you could be floating in a lifeboat for days before being rescued, you endeavour to save one book from the inky black depths. Which one would it be? For me it would be *Meditations* by Marcus Aurelius – no contest.

Written in a series of twelve notebooks, which were most likely never intended to be published, *Meditations* outlines Aurelius' thoughts on virtue, duty and spiritual well-being. Composed of beautiful epigrams and aphorisms, the meditations provide consolation, guidance and practical advice for decision-making, maintaining mindfulness and navigating life's ups and downs.

Widely regarded as one of the masterpieces of ancient philosophy and an important contribution to the philosophical practice of Stoicism, *Meditations* has influenced the lives and

thoughts of historical figures such as John Stuart Mill, Matthew Arnold, Frederick the Great of Russia and US President Bill Clinton. Although *100 Books to Live By* gives many suggestions for titles to help guide us, in truth you only really need to save one from the sinking ship. It's a medicine cabinet essential for when you are in need of wise words.

> *'The happiness of your life depends upon the quality of your thoughts: therefore guard accordingly, and take care that you entertain no notions unsuitable to virtue and reasonable nature.'*

CONDITION OR SITUATION:
When Life Feels at a Standstill

PRESCRIPTION:
Before the Coffee Gets Cold (2015)
by Toshikazu Kawaguchi

'At the end of the day, whether one returns to the past or travels to the future, the present doesn't change.'

Ever get the feeling that life is going nowhere? Ever feel that somewhere along life's journey you took the wrong road and found yourself in a cul-de-sac, and if only you could go back in time you would correct your direction?

Before the Coffee Gets Cold is a poignant and whimsical novel set in a small, timeless café in Tokyo called Funiculi Funicula. The café offers a unique opportunity: the chance to travel back in time, but with strict rules. Travellers must sit in a specific chair, they cannot leave the café during the journey, they must return before their coffee gets cold (a matter of minutes), and, most crucially, nothing they do in the past can change the present.

The novel is structured as a series of interconnected stories focusing on different characters who visit the café, each seeking to revisit a moment from their past as they struggle with regret – whether over unspoken words, missed opportunities or lost loved ones.

Each story unfolds with emotional depth as the characters confront their pasts or futures, learning to accept what cannot be changed while finding peace in the act of facing their regrets or unresolved emotions. The café serves as a magical yet grounded space where time's rigidity and human vulnerability collide, offering a tender exploration of love, loss and acceptance.

The novel's central conceit of time travel highlights both the longing to revisit or alter the past and the immutable nature of reality. The rule that the present cannot be changed underscores the importance of accepting life as it is, rather than being consumed by 'what ifs'. The act of revisiting the past allows the characters to seek emotional closure, even if the outcome remains unchanged, emphasizing to readers the healing power of acknowledgment over alteration.

Alternative Remedy:
Time Shelter (2022) by Bulgarian writer Georgi Gospodinov also uses time travel as a means of examining the past's relationship with the present, and is set against the backdrop of the treatment of Alzheimer's disease.

CONDITION OR SITUATION:
Chasing a Dream

PRESCRIPTION:
The Alchemist (1988)
by Paolo Coelho

*'When you want something, all the universe
conspires in helping you to achieve it.'*

Too often in life people hold back from doing what they want to, what they feel is their personal calling in life. Perhaps for fear of failure, perhaps because of obligations, perceived or otherwise. *The Alchemist* explores what it is to chase a dream.

The story follows a young shepherd named Santiago, who has a recurring dream about finding treasure at the pyramids in Egypt. Believing the dream to be a prophecy, Santiago embarks on a journey from his home in Spain to fulfil his destiny and find the treasure.

Along the way, Santiago meets various characters who guide or mislead him. He falls in love with a woman named Fatima, who becomes a significant figure in his journey. Santiago learns about alchemy, listens to the language of the universe, and comes to understand the concept of 'personal legend' – the unique destiny that each person has.

As Santiago travels through the desert he learns valuable lessons about listening to his heart and following his intuition. The novel is a philosophical exploration of self-discovery, spirituality and the importance of following one's dreams. Coelho explores the transformative power of love, as embodied by Santiago's love for Fatima. Their love is a source of inspiration and motivation for Santiago to continue his quest.

Santiago faces numerous challenges, and his journey is marked by uncertainty and risk, but he perseveres despite the many trials and setbacks in his way. In fact, he learns to embrace these difficulties as opportunities for growth, and remains committed to his 'personal legend'. So, the novel encourages readers to be open to new experiences and to view uncertainty as a natural part of the journey through life. It teaches the importance of resilience and determination in the face of adversity, and that we should trust our intuitions and follow our hearts.

Alternative Remedy:
The bestselling self-help book *The Four Agreements* (1997) by don Miguel Ruiz covers similar paths as *The Alchemist* by distilling the ancient spiritual wisdom of the Mexican Toltec culture into practical advice.

3

Remedies for the Mind

CONDITION OR SITUATION:
Feeling Existential Angst

PRESCRIPTION:
The Outsider (1942)

by Albert Camus

'I looked up at the mass of signs and stars in the night sky and laid myself open for the first time to the benign indifference of the world.'

Set in Algiers, *The Outsider* (*L'Étranger*) reflects on the absurdity and insignificance of human existence in an uncaring universe. Camus proposes that attempts to find meaning and purpose in life are all in vain, and that our actions and decisions are ultimately meaningless in the grand scheme of things.

The main character of the book, Meursault, is a disaffected young man who lacks an emotional connection with the world around him. The story begins with the death of his mother in a nursing home, and, after a chain of events, culminates with a senseless murder on a sun-drenched beach. This act was driven by a combination of factors, including the heat of the sun, the presence of Meursault's friends, and his own emotional detachment. *The Outsider* follows Meursault's trial and subsequent sentencing to death, which is the backdrop for his philosophical musings on the meaning of existence, morality and the ridiculousness of human life.

Raising the question of morality and ethics, *The Outsider* challenges the idea that there is a universal moral code that applies to all human beings and explores the tension between the individual and society and the ways in which social structures can constrain individual freedom and autonomy.

The Outsider forms a major keystone in Camus' philosophy of absurdism, which puts forward the argument that human existence is essentially meaningless, and that our attempts to find purpose and meaning in life are futile. This philosophy is built on the premise that such efforts are at odds with the fact that the universe is fundamentally indifferent to human existence.

Alternative Remedy:
For an equally bleak philosophical novel about suffering and the meaninglessness of life, try *Notes from Underground* (1864) by Fyodor Dostoevsky.

CONDITION OR SITUATION:
Falling on Hard Times

PRESCRIPTION:
Hunger (1899)
by Knut Hamsun

'I suffered no pain, my hunger had taken the edge off; instead I felt pleasantly empty, untouched by everything around me and happy to be unseen by all.'

It is often stated by homeless charities that we are all just a couple of bad decisions away from destitution. *Hunger* explores the physical and emotional struggles of a young, unnamed writer living in poverty in late nineteenth-century Oslo. The story follows the protagonist's descent into destitution as he navigates the city's streets, struggling to find food, shelter and meaning in his life.

The novel portrays the devastating impact of poverty on the human psyche, as the protagonist's hunger and desperation lead to feelings of shame, anxiety and despair. Hamsun also explores the tension between creativity and survival by showing the difficult balance between pursuing one's artistic passions and meeting basic survival needs. The protagonist's writing is often hindered by his physical and emotional struggles, illustrating the challenges of creating art in the face of adversity. In this sense the novel challenges the romanticized notion of the 'starving artist in a garret', and instead presents a stark, unflinching portrayal of the brutal realities of poverty. As the protagonist's hunger and desperation intensify, his grip on reality begins to slip, and he experiences episodes of hallucination, paranoia and disconnection from the world around him.

Hunger also examines the psychiatric phenomenon of self-sabotage. The protagonist gives away his food and clothes, refuses food he is offered and seems at times to be hell-bent on self-destruction. Hamsun shows the ways in which pride and ego can prevent individuals from seeking help, accepting support, and making positive changes in their lives.

Hunger suggests that addressing the underlying issues of poverty, such as lack of access to resources, education and job opportunities, is crucial for breaking the cycle of destitution and promoting long-term recovery. The book also emphasizes the importance of treating individuals struggling with poverty and self-sabotage with compassion, empathy and understanding, rather than with judgement or condemnation.

Alternative Remedy:
For an equally dark portrayal of social alienation and self-sabotage try *No Longer Human* (1948) by Japanese writer Osamu Dazai.

CONDITION OR SITUATION:
Feeling Out of Control

PRESCRIPTION:
Murphy (1938)
by Samuel Beckett

'The freedom of indifference, the indifference of freedom, the will dust in the dust of its object, the act a handful of sand let fall – these were some of the shapes he had sighted, sunset landfall after many days.'

Ever wonder about how much freedom and control we have over our lives? Some do so compulsively, and yearn to be separate – to escape the shackles of societal conformity. Literature is populated with anti-heroes undergoing such existential angst, but few have such tragicomic aplomb as the protagonist of Samuel Beckett's debut novel *Murphy*.

The story revolves around the titular character, a young Irishman living in London. Murphy is an outsider who rejects the conventions of society and seeks to escape the constraints of the world. He becomes obsessed with achieving a state of complete freedom and autonomy, which he believes can be attained through a process of self-isolation and withdrawal from society.

Through Murphy's experiences, Beckett highlights the illusion that humans have control over their lives. Despite his efforts to impose his own sense of order and structure on his life, he is constantly thwarted by external events and the unpredictability of the world. Paradoxically, however, Murphy's desire for autonomy and independence is accompanied by deep-seated fear and anxiety of the responsibilities and uncertainties that come with freedom. He is paralyzed by the infinite possibilities and choices that life presents, and he struggles to make decisions that will give his life meaning and direction.

Beckett's portrayal of Murphy's battle with the meaninglessness of life, the search for autonomy, and the illusion of control resonates with the existentialist philosophy of thinkers like Jean-Paul Sartre and Martin Heidegger. *Murphy* is characterized by its absurdity and humour, which serves to underscore the uncertainty of human existence. Beckett's heavy use of irony and pathos highlights the contradictions and paradoxes of human experience, and while it offers no answers to the ultimate questions, reading this masterpiece will leave you with a wry smile on your face.

Alternative Remedy:
A Confederacy of Dunces (1980) by John Kennedy Toole contains an equally disaffected protagonist struggling with concepts of social conformity, personal freedom and the illusion of control.

MEDICINE CABINET ESSENTIALS:
Crime and Punishment (1866)
by Fyodor Dostoevsky

Of all the novels categorized as psychological literary fiction, Dostoevsky's *Crime and Punishment* is possibly the apotheosis. The story follows Rodion Raskolnikov, a young and impoverished former student who murders an old pawnbroker and grapples with the consequences of his actions. *Crime and Punishment* explores the psychological motivations behind Raskolnikov's crime, as well as the emotional and psychological toll it takes on him.

The novel raises important questions about ethics, particularly in the context of Raskolnikov's utilitarian justification for the murder, which is rooted in his belief in a form of moral absolutism, that some individuals are above conventional moral norms. This is ultimately shown to be flawed and destructive. Raskolnikov's pride and ego lead him to think that he is above the law and that his crime is justified, but eventually, they contribute to his downfall.

Dostoevsky also explores the importance of human connection and empathy, particularly through the character of

Sonya, who is a source of compassion and understanding for Raskolnikov. Readers are treated to a description of a crushing weight of guilt and shame as Raskolnikov struggles with the emotional and psychological consequences of his actions and begins to confront his own flaws and weaknesses. His journey suggests that redemption is possible through personal suffering, self-reflection and taking responsibility for the exercise of free will.

Crime and Punishment is a rich and captivating novel that offers profound insights into the human condition. Through its exploration of the psychology of crime and guilt, morality and ethics, and redemption and personal growth, the novel provides an insightful and enlightening study of the complexities of human nature.

*'To go wrong in one's own way is better
than to go right in someone else's.'*

CONDITION OR SITUATION:
Struggling to Accept Difference

PRESCRIPTION:
Jonathan Livingston Seagull (1970)
by Richard Bach

'Look with your understanding, find out what you already know, and you'll see the way to fly.'

Ever feel different from the rest? Ever think that you don't really fit in with the people around you? Perhaps you have a different outlook on life or different beliefs and values than others? In this novella Richard Bach uses an allegory about a seabird flying away from the flock to instruct the reader on the importance of acceptance and difference.

Jonathan does not fit in with his flock. He is seen as different due to his pursuit of perfecting his flying skills, and his uniqueness is frowned upon by the other birds. However, this quest for perfection leads him to gain a deeper understanding of himself and the world in general, eventually realizing that his distinctiveness is a source of strength rather than weakness. Jonathan finally finds a community of like-minded seagulls who share his enthusiasm for flying, thus providing him with a sense of belonging and affirmation that was not given to him by his original flock.

Bach's telling of Jonathan's story encourages the reader to reflect on their own relationships with others and to nurture a more meaningful understanding and acceptance of those who may be different from themselves. Non-conformity, self-improvement and spirituality are all explored in this book, which advocates the importance of accepting and celebrating individuality and the uniqueness of other people. It also suggests that we look further than the conventions that rule our lives by embracing our own distinctive qualities and strengths.

Alternative Remedy:
For an alternative tale rich in allegory about loneliness, love and loss, and feeling different, try *The Little Prince* (1943) by Antoine de Saint-Exupéry.

CONDITION OR SITUATION:
Meditating on the Darkness of the Human Soul

PRESCRIPTION:
Heart of Darkness (1899)
by Joseph Conrad

'He cried in a whisper at some image, at some vision – he cried out twice, a cry that was no more than a breath: "The horror! The horror!"'

'If you gaze long into an abyss, the abyss gazes also into you,' wrote Friedrich Nietzsche, and this maxim is succinctly demonstrated by Joseph Conrad's novella that shows us the perils of contemplating the darkness of the human soul.

Heart of Darkness follows Marlow, a sailor who travels up the Congo River into the heart of Africa, in search of the infamous ivory trader Kurtz. The novella is a powerful exploration of the darker aspects of human nature. The character of Kurtz, in particular, represents the ultimate expression of this darkness, since he has descended into madness and savagery in the dark depths of the jungle.

Kurtz has become a symbol of power and authority, and he serves as a warning about the corrupting influence of power and the dangers of unchecked ambition. His character illustrates how power can lead individuals to abandon their moral principles and to engage in atrocities, and that it can ultimately consume and destroy them (Nietzsche's 'abyss').

The Heart of Darkness reveals that the capacity for cruelty, greed and violence is present in all individuals, and that it can be unleashed in the right circumstances. The novella also looks at the power of the unconscious mind, revealing the ways in which our deepest fears, desires and instincts can shape our actions and decisions. Conrad suggests that the unconscious is a force that cannot be fully controlled or understood, and that it can lead individuals down a path of destruction and chaos. The book serves as a warning about the dangers of gazing too 'long into an abyss'.

Alternative Remedy:
For another descent into the darkness of the human soul, try *Blood Meridian* (1985) by Cormac McCarthy, which deals with similar themes but in a gothic Western setting.

CONDITION OR SITUATION:
Being on a Journey of Self-Discovery

PRESCRIPTION:
The Magus (1965)
by John Fowles

> *'One kind of person is engaged in society without realizing it; another kind engages in society by controlling it.'*

It is often said that life is a journey of self-discovery, but that journey can take unexpected turns when we are least prepared. Take the case of Nicholas Urfe, the protagonist of *The Magus*. Disillusioned with his life and the drudgery of work, he decamps to the Greek island of Phraxos to 'find himself' and gets more than he bargained for as he becomes embroiled in a series of complex and mysterious psychological games.

At the core of *The Magus* is the tension between reality and illusion, as Nicholas becomes increasingly uncertain about what is real and what is part of the elaborate games being played out around him. Fowles examines the intricate power dynamics at play in relationships, particularly between Nicholas and the enigmatic Maurice Conchis, who orchestrates masques – bewildering theatrical playlets – also called 'the godgame'.

Through Nicholas' experiences, the novel illustrates the fragmented nature of identity and the ways in which our perceptions of ourselves and others are shaped by our experiences and relationships. Nicholas' journey is marked by uncertainty, confusion and discomfort, highlighting the challenges and difficulties that often accompany self-discovery. However Nicholas' experiences on Phraxos force him to confront his own biases and assumptions, leading to a deeper understanding of himself and the world around him.

The Magus shows the complexity and multiplicity of the self. Fowles suggests that a journey of self-discovery is not ultimately to find a destination, but rather a continuous voyage of exploration and learning, and that our understanding of ourselves is always subject to question, revision and refinement.

Alternative Remedy:
For another novel that examines the quest for knowledge and enlightenment using games as a metaphor, try Hermann Hesse's neo-science fiction novel *The Glass Bead Game* (1943).

CONDITION OR SITUATION:
Wanting to Understand the 'Quality' of Life

PRESCRIPTION:
Zen and the Art of Motorcycle Maintenance (1974)
by Robert M. Pirsig

'Quality ... you know what it is, yet you don't know what it is. But that's self-contradictory. But some things are better than others, that is, they have more quality.'

Pirsig's blend of fiction and non-fiction follows the motorcycle road trip made by Robert and his son Chris from Minnesota to northern California. At the same time it delves into various philosophical concepts, including Pirsig's idea of a philosophical structure he calls 'Metaphysics of Quality'.

The Metaphysics of Quality suggests to the reader that quality is a basic aspect of the reality that underlies all existence, arguing that Western philosophy has disregarded the concept of quality in our lives, but quality is necessary in order to understand the world and our experiences.

Finding a balance between different approaches to life, according to Pirsig, is essential to attaining a high degree of quality. This, along with the importance of self-reflection and introspection, is the key to understanding the world, attaining personal growth and improving the quality of your life.

It is recommended to the reader that care and attention should be taken in all aspects of life and Pirsig exemplifies this through the comparison with motorcycle maintenance, where the utmost care and attention to detail must be employed in order to ensure the quality of the motorcycle and to keep the rider safe.

Zen and the Art of Motorcycle Maintenance provides the reader with an interesting and thought-provoking enquiry into the meaning of quality and how it relates to our human experience.

Alternative Remedy:
For a lighter, entertaining introduction to Eastern philosophy try *The Tao of the Dude* (2015) by Oliver Benjamin, a book that takes the homespun wisdom of the protagonist of the Coen brothers' cult film *The Big Lebowski*, Jeffrey 'The Dude' Lebowski, and links it to Taoism. Some knowledge of the film is advised, however.

CONDITION OR SITUATION:
Struggling with Identity and Sense of Self

PRESCRIPTION:
Midnight's Children (1981)
by Salman Rushdie

'Memory's truth, because memory has its own special kind. It selects, eliminates, alters, exaggerates, minimizes, glorifies, and vilifies also; but in the end it creates its own reality.'

Salman Rushdie's *Midnight's Children* is a sweeping magical realist novel that interweaves the story of Saleem Sinai, born at the exact moment of India's independence, with India's emergence as a modern nation. The novel follows Saleem, who discovers he shares a mystical connection with the other children born in the first hour of India's independence, each possessing unique supernatural abilities.

In the story, Rushdie explores the intricate relationship between personal and national identity, particularly in the context of post-colonial India. The novel's scope encompasses partition, war, emergency rule under Indira Gandhi, and the countless social and political changes that shaped modern India. It tackles the legacy of colonialism and its impact on cultural identity. Through its rich tapestry of characters and events, it shows how Indian identity is inherently plural, hybrid and resistant to simple categorization. The fragmented narrative style mirrors this multiplicity, suggesting that both personal and national identities are necessarily complex and sometimes contradictory.

Rushdie masterfully employs magical realism to explore questions of truth, memory and identity. The novel suggests that both personal and national histories are constructed narratives, subject to distortion and reinterpretation. Through Saleem's often unreliable narration, Rushdie demonstrates how stories shape our understanding of ourselves and our place in the world.

Ultimately, the novel delivers a powerful message about the relationship between individual lives and historical forces. It suggests that while we are shaped by historical circumstances beyond our control, our individual stories and experiences contribute to the larger narrative of human experience. *Midnight's Children* celebrates the power of storytelling while acknowledging its limitations and affirms the importance of preserving individual voices within the grand sweep of history.

Alternative Remedy:
For another dose of magical realism and a discourse on the power of storytelling, try *The Shadow of The Wind* (2001) by Carlos Ruiz Zafón.

CONDITION OR SITUATION:
PTSD/Adult Trauma

PRESCRIPTION:
Slaughterhouse-Five (1969)
by Kurt Vonnegut

'And I asked myself about the present: how wide it was, how deep it was, how much was mine to keep.'

Post-traumatic stress disorder (PTSD) is a relatively recent identification of a mental condition, having been first formally diagnosed by the American Psychiatric Association in 1980. Literature, however, has a long history of describing similar conditions such as battle fatigue, combat trauma and shell shock, stretching back to Homer's *The Iliad*.

Slaughterhouse-Five tells the story of Billy Pilgrim, a World War II veteran who, as a prisoner of war, survived the Allied bombing of Dresden. Billy has become 'unstuck in time' because he has been kidnapped by an alien race called the Tralfamadorians. One of the principal themes of the novel pivots around fate and the illusion of control. The Tralfamadorians' concept of time, which sees all events as predetermined and unchangeable, raises questions about the nature of free will. This theme is expressed in Billy's own experiences, which often seem to be shaped by forces beyond his control.

Billy's non-linear experience of time, reflected in the narrative jumping backwards and forwards, allows Vonnegut to explore the fragmented and subjective nature of memory and the human experience. In addition, the novel's non-chronological structure mirrors the disjointed and often surreal nature of war.

The novel is a powerful anti-war statement, highlighting the senseless brutality and destruction caused by conflict. Vonnegut's depiction of the bombing of Dresden, which he himself witnessed, is a particularly striking example of the devastating and pointless atrocities of war. The consequences of trauma and violence can be long-lasting and far-reaching, and the book promotes the importance of acknowledging and addressing the impact of trauma on individuals and society, and of working towards a more compassionate and peaceful world.

Slaughterhouse-Five is a powerful and thought-provoking novel that challenges readers to think critically about the nature of war and violence, and the search for meaning and purpose in an often chaotic and unpredictable world.

Alternative Remedy:
For a slightly different take on the consequences of trauma that uses science fiction but has an eco-disaster as its catalyst, try *Annihilation* (2014) by Jeff VanderMeer.

MEDICINE CABINET ESSENTIALS:
Lolita (1955)
by Vladimir Nabokov

It is often said that love and hate aren't diametric opposites, but love and *indifference*, and that indifference to suffering can be a form of cruelty, a view that is brilliantly illustrated in *Lolita*. The book tells the disturbing story of Humbert Humbert, a middle-aged European intellectual who becomes infatuated with a twelve-year-old American girl named Dolores Haze, whom he nicknames 'Lolita'. Written as Humbert's confessional memoir from prison, the novel traces his journey of manipulation, abuse and moral decadence.

The central theme of *Lolita* is Humbert's obsessive and perverse desire for Lolita, which he frames as a tragic love story. Nabokov explores how obsession can distort reality, as Humbert's idealized vision of Lolita as a 'nymphet' blinds him to her youth, individuality and humanity. This theme critiques the romanticization of destructive desires and the ways in which individuals justify immoral actions.

Lolita also examines the dynamics of power and control in abusive relationships. Humbert exerts psychological and physical dominance over Lolita, exploiting her vulnerability as a child. His narration often glosses over her pain, revealing how

predators manipulate both their victims and their own self-perception to maintain control.

A multi-layered novel, *Lolita* is full of Nabokov's lush, lyrical prose and word play and offers a deeply unsettling perspective on love and cruelty, dismantling romantic ideals by showing how they can mask abuse. The book also exposes the insidious nature of cruelty through Humbert's justifications and Lolita's muted suffering. Humbert's cruelty is not just physical but psychological – he manipulates Lolita into accepting his actions while convincing himself (and attempting to convince the reader) that she is complicit or even seductive. Nabokov underscores the horror of this evil by occasionally allowing Lolita's pain to break through Humbert's narrative, such as in fleeting moments where her tears or resistance are mentioned. These glimpses remind readers that cruelty often hides behind self-delusion and charm, and if we listen and put aside our indifference we will notice and hear people's suffering:

> *'We had been everywhere. We had really seen nothing. And I catch myself thinking today that our long journey had only defiled with a sinuous trail of slime the lovely, trustful, dreamy, enormous country that by then, in retrospect, was no more to us than a collection of dog-eared maps, ruined tour books, old tires, and her sobs in the night – every night, every night – the moment I feigned sleep.'*

CONDITION OR SITUATION:
Conspiracy and Paranoia

PRESCRIPTION:
The Crying of Lot 49 (1966)
by Thomas Pynchon

'She knew you couldn't go backward. You had to go forward or sideways. The only way to stay in one place was to keep moving.'

The French situationist philosopher Guy Debord once commented on modern concerns with conspiracy theories that the question is not whether people are paranoid, but are they paranoid enough?

The Crying of Lot 49 follows the story of Oedipa Maas, a young woman living in California in the 1960s. The narrative begins when Oedipa is required to execute the will of her wealthy former lover, Pierce Inverarity. As Oedipa sorts through Pierce's vast estate, she becomes entangled in a mysterious quest to uncover the truth about a possible seventeenth-century conspiracy involving a secret postal system known as the Tristero.

Oedipa's investigation leads her down a rabbit hole of cryptic clues, obscure historical references and surreal experiences. She encounters a range of eccentric characters, from paranoid conspiracists to avant-garde artists, who all seem to be connected to the Tristero in some way. As Oedipa delves deeper into the mystery, she becomes increasingly obsessed with uncovering the truth, which may or may not be related to a real conspiracy.

Throughout the novel, Pynchon blurs the lines between reality and paranoia, leaving the reader questioning what is real and what is just Oedipa's perception. In fact, *The Crying of Lot 49* dismisses the notion of a single, objective truth. Instead, it presents a world where multiple narratives and interpretations coexist. By examining Oedipa's journey and the novel's complex narrative, readers can gain a deeper understanding of how conspiracy theories can captivate and unsettle individuals, often blurring the lines between reality and paranoia.

Pynchon suggests that conspiracy theories can be a reflection of deeper societal anxieties and fears. The Tristero conspiracy taps into Oedipa's (and the reader's) anxieties about the nature of reality, control and the search for meaning.

Alternative Remedy:
Another novel that plays around with alternate multiple realities is *The Invention of Morel* (1940) by Argentine writer Adolfo Bioy Casares. The story concerns a fugitive hiding on a desert island where all is not what it seems.

CONDITION OR SITUATION:
Living with the Trauma of Conflict

PRESCRIPTION:
The General of the Dead Army (1963)
by Ismail Kadare

'I have a whole army of dead men under my command now, he thought. Only instead of uniforms they are all wearing nylon bags. Blue bags with two white stripes ...'

Albanian writer Ismail Kadare's satirical novel revolves around an unnamed Italian general who is sent to Albania to oversee the exhumation and repatriation of the remains of Italian soldiers who died during World War I. The general's journey becomes a personal quest as he grapples with the purpose of his mission and the significance of his own existence. Through the general's experiences, Kadare explores the human search for identity, purpose and meaning in a post-war world.

The novel is also a satire of bureaucratic red tape and the absurdities of officialdom as the general has to struggle with both the Albanian authorities and the Italian military hierarchy. The bleak farce of the general's predicament is a counterpoint to an exploration of the tension between modernity and tradition, with the general's modern, industrialized world clashing with the traditional old world of rural Albania. Pervading the narrative is the theme of the power of the past and how it continues to shape lives. In particular, the legacy of conflict can haunt individuals and societies for generations, and the general's encounters with the Albanian people and landscape serve as a reminder of the enduring impact of historical events.

The novel ultimately presents a bleak and pessimistic view of human nature, highlighting the absurdities and cruelties of war and the dehumanizing effects of bureaucratic systems. However, although we cannot escape the past and its influence on the present, *The General of the Dead Army* shows us that it is essential to confront and understand historical events in order to move forward.

Alternative Remedy:
For another gritty account of the traumas of conflict and the dehumanization caused by war, try *The Naked and The Dead* (1948) by Norman Mailer, based on the author's experiences of serving in the US Army in World War II.

CONDITION OR SITUATION:
Facing the Inevitability of Death

PRESCRIPTION:
As I Lay Dying (1930)
by William Faulkner

*'The reason for living was to get ready
to stay dead a long time.'*

Contemplating one's own mortality can occur at any point in life and after any incident, from surviving a near-death experience to coping with the loss of a close family member. *As I Lay Dying* takes the latter scenario and uses it as the focal point of a philosophical treatise on human mortality. The story revolves around the Bundren family, who embark on a journey to bury their matriarch, Addie, in her hometown of Jefferson, Mississippi. The novel is told through multiple voices, each with their own unique perspective and biases, which creates a complex and fragmented narrative.

Faulkner begins the story of *As I Lay Dying* with Addie's death, and on the family's journey, the family faces numerous challenges including a flooded river, a broken wagon, and their own personal struggles to come to terms with their grief. Each chapter explores the inner lives and thoughts of a different character, revealing their motivations, desires and conflicts.

The central message of the novel is that life and death are inextricably linked, and that death is a natural part of the human experience. The novel suggests that death is not an end, but rather a transformation, and that it can be a catalyst for growth, change and self-discovery. Ultimately, the novel tells us that life is precious and fleeting, and that we must make the most of the time we have. The novel's famous one-line chapter, 'My mother is a fish,' is a powerful expression of this idea, suggesting that even in death, there is a kind of transformation, renewal and rebirth.

Alternative Remedy:
For another meditation on mortality try *Last Orders* (1996) by Graham Swift, a novel that bears more than a passing resemblance to *As I Lay Dying*.

CONDITION OR SITUATION:
Contemplating the Enigma of Time and Mortality

PRESCRIPTION:
The Life and Times of Michael K (1983)
by J. M. Coetzee

'In the end, it's not the years in your life that count, it's the life in your years.'

Have you noticed that as you get older time seems to speed up? The summer holidays seemed to last an eternity when you were young, but the older you get, the faster they flash by. It is not uncommon to be gripped by a curious anxiety and start to count how many summers we might have left.

The Life and Times of Michael K tells the story of a simple but enigmatic man who embarks on a journey through a war-torn South Africa. The novel explores several themes, including the search for identity, the effects of war and violence, and the human condition. However, at its core, it is a profound meditation on time and mortality.

The novel highlights the fragility of human existence.

Michael K's journey is marked by death, violence and decay, which serve as a reminder of the transience of human life. Coetzee highlights the ways in which time is both a source of meaning and a force of destruction. As Michael navigates the desolate landscape of the war-torn country, he is constantly reminded of the impermanence of all things.

Michael's experiences are marked by a sense of disconnection from the world, and he often finds himself at odds with the societal norms and expectations that govern the lives of those around him. Through Michael's character, Coetzee suggests that time is not an objective reality, but rather a human construct that is shaped by our experiences, perceptions and cultural norms. This theme is reinforced by the novel's non-linear narrative structure, which blurs the boundaries between past, present and future through flashbacks to past events and Michael's musings on the future.

The Life and Times of Michael K offers a profound exploration of the human condition, and encourages readers to confront the complexities and mysteries of time as well as the reality of our own mortality.

Alternative Remedy:
Another novel from a very different genre of fiction (science fiction) that deals with time, mortality and the impermanence of things is *Never Let Me Go* (2005) by Kazuo Ishiguro.

CONDITION OR SITUATION:
Distinguishing the Difference between Appearance and Reality

PRESCRIPTION:
The Secret History (1992)
by Donna Tartt

'Does such a thing as "the fatal flaw", that showy dark crack running down the middle of a life, exist outside of literature? I used to think it didn't.'

We are living in a post-truth world, bombarded with AI-altered realities and deepfake representations where it becomes increasingly difficult to tell what is real from what is bogus, and merely made to appear real. *The Secret History* is a complex and thought-provoking exploration of the darker aspects of human nature, morality and the blurred lines between appearance and reality. The story follows a group of privileged college students who commit a murder, and the novel's layered, intricate narrative slowly unravels the events leading up to the crime and the consequences that follow.

The novel centres around Richard Papen, a young man from a working-class family in California, who gains admission to Hampden College, a prestigious liberal arts college in

New England. Richard becomes infatuated with a group of classmates who are studying under the charismatic and demanding Professor Julian Morrow. As the story unfolds, the group's dynamics become increasingly complicated, and they become embroiled in the tragic event that changes their lives forever.

The novel satirizes the elitist culture that pervades the characters' world, highlighting the dangers of exclusivity and the assumption of superiority. Richard's narrative is inherently unreliable, as he is both a participant in and an observer of the events that unfold. This unreliability forces readers to question the accuracy of the narrative and to piece together the truth for themselves.

The Secret History is a masterful exploration of the tension between appearance and reality. Tartt expertly peels back the layers of her characters' personas, revealing the dark underbelly of their privileged lives. She teaches us that appearances can be deceptive and that the truth is often hidden beneath the surface.

Alternative Remedy:
For another delicious delve into the pathology of elitism and an exploration of the tension between appearance and reality (with a wholly unreliable narrator) try *The Debt to Pleasure* (1996) by John Lanchester – a novel written mainly in three-course menu recipes.

MEDICINE CABINET ESSENTIALS:
The Tin Drum (1959)
by Günter Grass

Every bibliophile has a list of what they consider to be the greatest books they have ever read, books that have moved them in profound ways, taught them important life lessons or that were just mind-blowing works of the imagination that carried them away to a different world. For me, *The Tin Drum* fits into this latter category: it is a novel so bewilderingly strange and macabre it left an indelible stamp upon my mind.

The Tin Drum tells the story of Oskar Matzerath, a young boy who decides to stop growing at the age of three, and narrates recollections of his life in pre- and post-war Germany. Each chapter in this sprawling novel is like an individual short story or set piece scene which Oskar recounts with grisly glee as we encounter a cast of bizarre characters and outlandish situations. A major theme is an exploration of the complexities of German identity and history, particularly in the context of the rise of Nazism and the aftermath of World War II. Oskar's narrative raises questions about the nature of innocence and guilt, especially in the Nazi era.

The novel's main message is that the world has gone crazy, and that the norms and values of society have been turned upside down. Through Oskar's eyes, we see a world that is increasingly absurd, chaotic and morally bankrupt. The rise of Nazism and the horrors committed during World War II are presented as a manifestation of this madness, and the novel critiques the complicity and silence of ordinary Germans in the face of these atrocities.

Oskar's narrative is a complex web of twisted recollections, myths and fantasies that blur the lines between reality and fiction, foregrounding the power of storytelling and memory to shape our understanding of ourselves and our world. *The Tin Drum* is a beguiling work of art: funny and sad, disquieting and enlightening, filled with many memorable images that linger long in the mind after you have turned over the last page. This is a book to read when it seems the whole world has gone crazy, for, as Oskar wryly observes in the opening line of his memoir, 'Granted: I am an inmate of a mental institution.'

> *'Even bad books are books*
> *and therefore sacred.'*

CONDITION OR SITUATION:
Feeling Baffled by the Illogical Paradoxes of Life

PRESCRIPTION:
Catch-22 (1961)
by Joseph Heller

'The enemy is anybody who's going to get you killed, no matter which side he's on, and that includes Colonel Cathcart. And don't you forget that, because the longer you remember it, the longer you might live.'

Sometimes the systems that govern our lives look as if they have been arbitrarily imposed, seemingly not to help us but to hinder us. These things are sent to try us! But often a very clear paradox seems blindingly obvious, yet nothing ever changes, as in Joseph Heller's satirical novel *Catch-22*. This is the story of Captain John Yossarian, a US Air Force bombardier stationed on the island of Pianosa during World War II. The book is a complex and absurd exploration of the illogical and bureaucratic systems that govern military life, as well as more general human affairs.

The story centres around the concept of 'Catch-22', a fictional military regulation that creates a paradoxical and impossible situation for airmen. According to *Catch-22*, any pilot who is deemed insane can be relieved of duty. However, in order to be declared insane, a pilot must request a psychiatric evaluation. But, by requesting a psychiatric evaluation, the pilot is demonstrating a rational concern for their safety, and therefore, cannot be considered insane. 'Catch-22' is a classic example of the liar paradox, where a statement is self-contradictory and cannot be either true or false.

As Yossarian confronts the follies of military bureaucracy, he becomes increasingly disillusioned with the system and the war effort. He is surrounded by a cast of characters, including his fellow airmen, officers and bureaucrats, who are all trapped in their own ways by the illogical and contradictory rules that govern their lives.

Catch-22 is a scathing critique of the absurdity of bureaucracy, highlighting the ways in which bureaucratic systems can become self-perpetuating and illogical. The concept of 'Catch-22' itself is a perfect example of how rules can be self-contradictory, creating paradoxes and impossible situations for individuals and trapping them in a cycle of farce and frustration.

Alternative Remedy:
The absurdity of military bureaucracy is beautifully exposed in Jaroslav Hašek's dark comic masterpiece *The Good Soldier Švejk* (1921–23).

CONDITION OR SITUATION:
Wanting to Inspire Resistance and Rebellion

PRESCRIPTION:
One Flew Over the Cuckoo's Nest (1962)
by Ken Kesey

'His whole body shakes with the strain as he tries to lift something he knows he can't lift, something everybody knows he can't lift. But, for just a second, when we hear the cement grind at our feet, we think, by golly, he might do it.'

Focusing on rebellion and resistance, and the importance of challenging authority, *One Flew Over the Cuckoo's Nest* is set in the 1950s in a psychiatric hospital, and the story is told by Chief Bromden, a long-term patient who is seemingly deaf and mute. Nurse Ratched is in charge of the ward and controls the patients with intimidation, manipulation and drugs, ruling out any possible dissent. That is until the arrival of a new patient, Randle McMurphy, a strong, confident character, who sets about questioning and challenging Nurse Ratched's authority, disrupting the hospital's routine.

As McMurphy encourages other patients to question her

rules, Ratched becomes determined to stamp out resistance, and their struggle culminates when McMurphy realizes that the patients' mental illnesses are not as severe as they are purported to be. This raises questions as to the definition of 'crazy' and who is in a position to define it.

Rather than blindly accepting the rules and norms that authority lays down for us, the novel encourages readers to question the status quo and challenge it, as a powerful pathway to creating change. It also highlights the hazards of unchecked power and the ways in which those in control can use manipulation and coercion to preserve their authority.

Kesey also focuses on the importance of human connection and relationships in making positive changes and advancing personal growth. Due to McMurphy's interaction with them, the patients come to realize how they have been controlled by Ratched, allowing them to see the injustices imposed by her.

One Flew Over the Cuckoo's Nest shows how taking risks and challenging authority can help bring about positive changes. It also focuses on the importance of keeping one's individuality despite the pressure to conform.

Alternative Remedy:
Another book that dives right into the 1960s counterculture and is just about as rebellious and 'sticking it to the man' as you can get, is Hunter S. Thompson's *Fear and Loathing in Las Vegas* (1971).

CONDITION OR SITUATION:
Struggling to Move On

PRESCRIPTION:
Nausea (1938)
by Jean-Paul Sartre

'I am no longer free, I can no longer do what I will.'

It is not uncommon in life at some point or other to feel stuck in a rut, that life is passing us by. It is at these points of inertia that it is also not uncommon to question if life has any real meaning beyond drudgery and despair. This is the position Antoine Roquentin finds himself in Jean-Paul Sartre's debut novel *Nausea*.

Roquentin, a sullen and brooding intellectual, has been living in the fictional seaside town of Bouville for several years but has failed to forge any meaningful friendships. Written in the form of a diary or notebook, the novel delves into concepts of existence, freedom and the inherent meaninglessness of life. Roquentin grapples with the idea that human existence is not predetermined, and that we must take responsibility for creating our own meaning.

The novel explores the differences between the individual's subjective experience and the objective world. Roquentin's perceptions of reality are constantly shifting, highlighting the provisional nature of human understanding. Throughout a long, bleak winter, Roquentin begins to experience a creeping sense of disgust at the people and things around him and in the things that he does; this revulsion he calls 'the nausea'. Through Roquentin's struggles, Sartre illustrates the concept of 'bad faith' (*mauvaise foi*), where individuals deny or escape their freedom, and the importance of acknowledging and accepting responsibility for one's choices.

The novel's exploration of existential ideas will prompt you to examine your own values, beliefs and assumptions about the world. By confronting themes of freedom, responsibility and the absurdity of life, you may be motivated to re-evaluate your priorities and goals, leading to a more purposeful life.

Alternative Remedy:
For a clear evocation of the essential absurdity of looking for abstract meaning in life, try Albert Camus' non-fiction essay *The Myth of Sisyphus* (1942).

CONDITION OR SITUATION:
Accepting Things as They Are

PRESCRIPTION:
The Sea, The Sea (1978)
by Iris Murdoch

'You seem to think the past is unreal, a pit full of ghosts. But to me the past is in some ways the most real thing of all.'

Throughout parts of this book I find myself musing on the importance of self-awareness and self-knowledge and the power of literature to provoke self-reflection (see the Introduction). But can too much self-reflection be a bad thing? At what point does healthy meditation on one's thought processes and actions start to descend into vainglorious and complacent self-absorption? The ancient Greeks had a wonderful word for this: *omphaloskepsis*, from *omphalós*, meaning the navel, and *sképsis,* meaning to examine or to contemplate. This gives us the literal English translation of 'contemplation of one's navel'. Iris Murdoch's *The Sea, The Sea*, winner of the Booker Prize in 1978, is basically a 500-p. illustration of the folly of too much navel-gazing.

The story follows Charles Arrowby, a former theatre director who has decided to escape the chaos of London and retire to a remote coastal village to write his memoirs. While there he has a chance encounter with his first love and this sends him spiralling into a mental whirlpool of self-absorption and delusions about his past.

Charles' interactions with the people around him are a masterclass in awkwardness, highlighting the ways in which humans can be both cruel and kind to each other, often simultaneously.

The Sea, The Sea explores the dangers of nostalgia. Charles' obsession with his past loves and losses serves as a warning about the perils of getting stuck in the past and neglecting the present. The novel shows the ways in which relationships can be both intense and ephemeral, reminding us to appreciate the people and experiences in our lives while they're still present, and to accept things as they are rather than lamenting what wasn't to be.

Alternative Remedy:
For another witty dose of extreme self-delusion by an unreliable narrator with literary pretensions, try *Pale Fire* (1962) by Vladimir Nabokov.

4

Remedies for the Self and Others

CONDITION OR SITUATION:
Loss of Innocence/Coming of Age

PRESCRIPTION:
To Kill a Mockingbird (1960)
by Harper Lee

*'Shoot all the bluejays you want, if you can hit 'em,
but remember it's a sin to kill a mockingbird.'*

The Pulitzer Prize-winning novel *To Kill a Mockingbird* is set in the fictional town of Maycomb, Alabama, during the Great Depression. The story is narrated by Scout, a young girl who recounts her childhood experiences alongside her older brother, Jem, and their father, Atticus Finch, a widowed lawyer.

The novel spans three years, following Atticus' legal defence of Tom Robinson, a Black man falsely accused of raping a white woman, despite knowing the case is unwinnable due to the town's ingrained racism.

The story is a coming-of-age narrative that focuses on Scout and Jem's growing understanding of their community's deep-seated racial prejudice. Scout and Jem confront the harsh realities of the adult world, shedding their childhood innocence. Their exposure to hatred, injustice and violence forces them to face up to the imperfections of their community and the moral compromises people make.

The loss of innocence in the novel is depicted as a gradual, layered process rather than a single moment, although for Jem, the trial's outcome is a shattering blow. His emotional reaction – anger and disillusionment – marks a deeper, more cynical shift as he struggles to reconcile his belief in justice with reality. Scout, younger and more sheltered by Atticus' explanations, experiences this loss more slowly. She learns that good can exist alongside evil, but it often requires personal risk and is not always recognized or rewarded.

Lee suggests that the loss of innocence, while painful, is necessary for moral growth and empathy. Scout and Jem's disillusionment enables them to develop a more nuanced understanding of human nature and to adopt Atticus' principle of empathy – seeing the world from others' perspectives. For readers, this teaches that confronting harsh truths, such as inequality and cruelty, is a critical step toward becoming compassionate, engaged individuals who can challenge injustice rather than passively accept it.

Alternative Remedy:
For a more contemporary novel that explores ingrained racism in the deep south of America try *Mudbound* (2008) by Hillary Jordan.

CONDITION OR SITUATION:
Growing Pains/Adolescent Angst

PRESCRIPTION:
The Catcher in the Rye (1951)
by J. D. Salinger

'I'm just going through a phase right now. Everybody goes through phases and all, don't they?'

Everyone goes through the pains of adolescence: raging hormones, feeling disillusioned and that nobody understands you, fearing that your fragile ego will be exposed at any moment. It's all part of the growing pains of leaving adolescence and joining the adult world. In short, it sucks! But be assured you are not alone. Take the case of Holden Caulfield, protagonist of J. D. Salinger's coming-of-age novel *The Catcher in the Rye*.

The story recounts a few days Holden spends wandering around New York City after being expelled from his boarding school. Instead of immediately going home to face his parents, he decides to stay in New York, experiencing a sense of freedom mixed with intense loneliness and alienation. He attempts to connect with various people – former teachers, old friends, a prostitute, nuns and eventually his younger sister, Phoebe.

However, most of his interactions are awkward, superficial or end in disillusionment. A central theme is Holden's profound feeling of being disconnected from others and society. Despite being surrounded by people in New York, he struggles to make genuine relationships and often feels misunderstood and alone.

Holden is obsessed with identifying 'phonies' – people he sees as artificial, pretentious or hypocritical. This reflects his search for true, honest connections in a world he perceives as superficial and corrupt. The novel explores the painful transition from childhood innocence to the complexities and perceived corruption of adulthood. Holden idealizes childhood purity and desperately wants to protect it, particularly in his sister Phoebe. The title metaphor, 'the catcher in the rye', symbolizes his fantasy of saving children from falling off the cliff into the adult world.

The Catcher in the Rye tells teenagers that feeling disillusioned with the world and the people in it is not uncommon during this stage of life. The book gives voice to the critical, often cynical, perspective that can develop as one begins to see the flaws in society and adults.

Alternative Remedy:
For a modern take on the coming-of-age novel exploring the pains of adolescence try *The Perks of Being a Wallflower* (1999) by Stephen Chbosky.

CONDITION OR SITUATION:
Fostering Self-Knowledge

PRESCRIPTION:
Pride and Prejudice (1813)
by Jane Austen

*'It is very often nothing but our
own vanity that deceives us.'*

We are all guilty from time to time of making snap judgements from predisposed opinions or mistaken intuitions. We may aspire to the adage of not judging a book by its cover, but we often do, nonetheless, and the important thing is to try to learn from our errors of judgement by fostering self-knowledge. One of the principal concerns of Jane Austen's timeless novel is the dangers of making judgements based on first impressions, as exemplified by the titular pride and prejudices of Elizabeth Bennet and Mr Darcy. Through their gradual realization of their own biases and misconceptions, Austen highlights the importance of self-awareness, humility and open-mindedness in personal relationships.

The novel also explores the theme of personal growth and development, as Elizabeth and Darcy navigate their flaws and weaknesses in order to become better versions of themselves.

Austen shows how both characters must confront their own pride and prejudices in order to achieve a deeper understanding of themselves and each other, and to find happiness together.

Austen's novel serves as a withering critique of the social conventions and expectations that govern the lives of her characters. She slyly pokes fun at the absurdities of the class system, particularly in her portrayal of characters such as Mr Collins and Lady Catherine de Bourgh, who embody the worst excesses of snobbery and social status. At the same time, Austen offers a nuanced exploration of the limited options available to women in a society where marriage was often the only means of securing financial stability.

Pride and Prejudice is a novel about the importance of social morality and of examining and fostering self-knowledge, as well as looking at the need for individuals to take responsibility for their own actions.

Alternative Remedy:
For a different perspective on the events of *Pride and Prejudice*, Jo Baker's 2013 novel *Longbourn* explores Jane Austen's world through the eyes of one of the servants at the Bennet family home.

MEDICINE CABINET ESSENTIALS:
If This Is a Man (1947)
by Primo Levi

One philosophical question about books and literature in particular is: are there subjects too horrific to properly evoke in words? Is it possible to describe the indescribable? *If This Is a Man* is a memoir by Primo Levi, an Italian Jewish chemist and writer, who survived the Auschwitz concentration camp during World War II. The book, first published in 1947, is a powerful and poignant account of Levi's experiences in the camp, focusing on humanity and inhumanity in the face of extreme suffering. It does indeed describe the indescribable.

The book's central message is that the Nazi regime's attempt to dehumanize and destroy the prisoners was not only a physical, but also a moral and spiritual assault. Levi argues that the camp's brutal conditions, the constant struggle for survival, and the erosion of dignity and identity threatened to reduce the prisoners to a state of 'non-men', stripping them of their humanity. Through his own experiences and observations, Levi shows how the prisoners were forced to confront the darkest aspects of human nature, including cruelty, violence and the collapse of moral values.

One of the most significant aspects of the book is Levi's

exploration of the 'grey zone', a concept he introduces to describe the moral ambiguity and complexity of life in the camp. This grey zone is characterized by a blurring of ethical boundaries, where prisoners were forced to collaborate with their oppressors or engage in behaviours that would be considered unacceptable in normal circumstances. Levi argues that the prisoners were not simply victims or heroes, but rather individuals who were forced to make difficult choices and compromises in order to survive.

Through his writing, Levi conveys the importance of preserving human dignity, even in the most extreme and dehumanizing conditions. He shows how the prisoners found ways to resist, to maintain their sense of self, and to hold on to their humanity, often through small acts of defiance, solidarity and cultural expression.

If This Is a Man is a testament to the human spirit's capacity for resilience, hope and survival, even in the face of unimaginable horror and suffering. Readers will be deeply moved and challenged by Levi's account, and will emerge with a deeper understanding of the importance of compassion, moral responsibility and valuing the sanctity of human life.

> *'In history and in life one sometimes seems to glimpse a ferocious law which states: "To he that has, will be given; from he that has not, will be taken away."'*

CONDITION OR SITUATION:
Gaining Strength through Solidarity

PRESCRIPTION:
Germinal (1885)
by Émile Zola

'Men were springing forth, a black avenging army, germinating slowly in the furrows, growing towards the harvests of the next century, and their germination would soon overturn the earth.'

Émile Zola's novel *Germinal* recounts the story of the struggles of coal miners in northern France during the late nineteenth century. The novel is set against the backdrop of the miners' strike and explores the harsh realities of their lives, including poverty, exploitation and the struggle for survival. Zola exposes the brutal treatment of miners by their employers, highlighting the long hours, low wages and hazardous working conditions they endure.

Germinal presents a withering criticism of the excesses of capitalism, demonstrating how the pursuit of profit can lead to the exploitation and suffering of the working class. The character of Monsieur Hennebeau, the pit owner's representative, embodies the callousness and greed of the capitalist class.

Zola also explores the clash of individual desires and the needs of the collective, highlighting the difficulties of balancing personal interests with the greater good. The character of Étienne is torn between his own wishes and his commitment to the strike. The novel demonstrates the strength and solidarity of the miners as they come together to demand better working conditions and fair wages. The character of Souvarine, a Russian anarchist, plays a key role in organizing the strike and rallying the miners to the cause. However, Souvarine preaches violent revolt and ultimately this leads to the riot that causes the strike to fail.

Zola ends the novel on a note of optimism. He suggests that, ultimately, when individuals form a collective and seek change, they can achieve great things and create a better future for themselves and their communities.

Alternative Remedy:
For an English view of the plight of the working class and the inequalities and excesses of capitalist exploitation try *The Ragged Trousered Philanthropists* (1914) by Robert Tressell, a novel George Orwell declared 'everyone should read'.

CONDITION OR SITUATION:
Finding Strength to Fight the Patriarchy

PRESCRIPTION:
Nervous Conditions (1988)
by Tsitsi Dangarembga

'You are one of the rare people who can separate your observation from your perception ... you see what is, where most people see what they expect.'

Narrated by Tambudzai (Tambu), *Nervous Conditions* tells the story of a young Shona girl living in rural Rhodesia (now Zimbabwe) during the 1960s and 1970s, and her struggle to reconcile the conflicting societal norms of Shona culture and Western ideals. This conflict is also coupled with coping with the presence of patriarchy in both societies, making her efforts to find her identity all the more difficult. Eventually this leads to mental illness.

Tambu grows up in a traditional Shona family, so her brother is the only one expected to be educated, as is customary in the patriarchal society. However, when he suddenly dies, Tambu gets the chance to take his place at the mission school and goes to live with her uncle Babamukuru, a well-educated Westernized man, and his family, whose lives are shaped by colonial education and values that are very different to her own.

Obtaining a Western education opens Tambu's eyes to the injustices imposed upon women in both Shona society, where women like her mother are often silenced by patriarchal norms, and under colonial structures, as she experiences her uncle's authoritarian rule over the family.

Tambu's search for identity while living up to conflicting cultural and social expectations of both patriarchal societies causes her to experience eating disorders and, as the title suggests, nervous conditions.

However, the novel highlights to the reader that despite systemic barriers, women can find the resilience and fortitude to combat patriarchal oppression. The book also teaches us to recognize and empathize with those who carry the burden of historical and cultural repression.

Alternative Remedy:
For another withering criticism of African patriarchy try *Woman at Point Zero* (1975) by Nawal El Saadawi. Based on the true story of a prostitute on death row for murdering her pimp, the book was initially banned in El Saadawi's native Egypt.

CONDITION OR SITUATION:
Coming of Age

PRESCRIPTION:
Norwegian Wood (1987)
by Haruki Murakami

'No truth can cure the sorrow we feel from losing a loved one. No truth, no sincerity, no strength, no kindness can cure that sorrow. All we can do is see it through to the end and learn something from it, but what we learn will be no help in facing the next sorrow that comes to us without warning.'

With a title inspired by The Beatles' song, *Norwegian Wood* is set in 1960s Tokyo against the backdrop of student protests and a changing Japanese society. It is told retrospectively by Toru Watanabe, a young man reflecting on his time at university and the emotional uncertainty and turmoil he experienced during these years.

The story describes Toru's relationships with two contrasting young women. First there is Naoko, the girlfriend of his late best friend Kizuki, who committed suicide. As a result, Naoko struggles with depression and mental illness, leaving her fragile and vulnerable. Then there is Midori, a vibrant and outspoken classmate. Toru's reflections on the nature of his feelings suggest that love is not always straightforward and that relationships need to be approached with patience and empathy.

He also looks back on the pain he faced in dealing with the grief of losing a friend, and considers the complexity of human connections as he searches for meaning in a transient world.

Toru's exploration of his youth follows his coming of age and the wisdom gained over time from painful experiences, as well as the realization of life's impermanence. The novel encourages readers to reflect on how their own past experiences of both pain and happiness shape their individual identity, and Murakami advocates that readers appreciate both the beauty and the sadness they encounter, which can lead to a deeper appreciation of human relationships.

Alternative Remedy:
Another contemporary Japanese novel that explores youthful troubles, but with a focus on bullying in adolescence, is *Heaven* (2009) by Mieko Kawakami.

CONDITION OR SITUATION:
Doubting the Power of Perseverance

PRESCRIPTION:
The Old Man and the Sea (1952)
by Ernest Hemingway

"'But man is not made for defeat,' he said. 'A man can be destroyed but not defeated.'"

Sometimes in life we find ourselves engulfed by an ocean of frustrations. Things just don't work out how we want them to, no matter how hard we try, and there is a strong temptation to simply throw in the towel and give up. It is at this point we should recall the struggles of Ernest Hemingway's salty old sea dog in the novella *The Old Man and The Sea*. The story follows the journey of an aging fisherman, Santiago, who embarks on a solo voyage in the Gulf Stream to catch a giant marlin.

Santiago's journey is a testament to the power of perseverance and determination. Despite his advanced age and the challenges he faces, he refuses to give up, and his determination ultimately leads to his triumph. Hemingway explores concepts of courage and bravery, pride and humility, as Santiago faces his fears and pushes himself to the limit to catch the marlin. His bravery is not just physical, but also emotional, as he confronts his own mortality and the meaning of his life. Santiago's pride is both his greatest strength and his greatest weakness. His pride drives him to catch the marlin, but it also leads him to underestimate the power of nature. Pride therefore can be a double-edged sword, and humility is essential for achieving true fulfilment in life.

The Old Man and the Sea highlights the eternal struggle between humans and nature. Santiago's battle with the marlin is a metaphor for the human condition, as he struggles to impose his will on the natural world. His story teaches us that with determination and perseverance, we can overcome even the most daunting challenges.

Alternative Remedy:
For the ultimate expression of humans locked in a battle to the death with the ravages of the natural world try *Moby-Dick* (1851) by Herman Melville.

MEDICINE CABINET ESSENTIALS:
Great Expectations (1861)
by Charles Dickens

This classic coming-of-age novel, *Great Expectations*, follows the life of Philip Pirrip, commonly known as Pip, an orphan living in rural England. The story begins when, as a young boy, Pip encounters an escaped convict, Abel Magwitch, in a graveyard. Pip helps the convict by stealing food and a file for him, an act that sets the course of his life in unexpected ways.

Pip's life first changes dramatically when he is invited to the home of the wealthy, eccentric Miss Havisham, a woman who was jilted at the altar and lives frozen in time, surrounded by the decaying remnants of her wedding day. There, Pip meets Estella, Miss Havisham's beautiful but cold-hearted adopted daughter, and becomes infatuated with her.

One of the central themes of *Great Expectations* is a critique of social hierarchy and the pursuit of status. Pip's desire to rise above his humble origins reflects the Victorian obsession with class mobility, but Dickens shows how this ambition can lead to alienation, ingratitude and moral corruption. The novel questions whether true worth lies in wealth and status or in character and kindness.

Dickens explores the corrupting influence of wealth through Pip's transformation after receiving his fortune. Pip initially equates money with happiness and superiority, but his journey reveals that wealth can isolate and distort one's values. Characters like Magwitch, who finds redemption through generosity, contrast with others like Miss Havisham, whose wealth breeds bitterness.

The title itself is a reminder that unrealistic hopes – whether for love, success or status – can lead to disillusionment. The novel encourages us to ground our aspirations in reality and appreciate what we have. Pip learns too late that wealth and status cannot replace the love and loyalty of family and friends, so *Great Expectations* teaches us to prioritize relationships and inner character over external achievements and material wealth and status.

> *'I am not at all happy as I am. I am disgusted with my calling and with my life.'*

CONDITION OR SITUATION:
Integrity in the Face of Injustice and Corruption

PRESCRIPTION:
The Beautyful Ones Are Not Yet Born (1968)
by Ayi Kwei Armah

'Alone, I am nothing. I have nothing. We have power. But we will never know it, we will never see it work. Unless we come together to make it work.'

Set in post-independence Ghana during the 1960s, the story follows an unnamed protagonist, often referred to as 'the man', who works as a railway clerk in a corrupt and rotting society. The man struggles to maintain his ethical integrity in a world rife with bribery and moral decay. He faces pressure from his family and society to compromise his principles for material gain, while his encounters with corrupt officials, exploitative systems and disillusioned friends highlight the pervasive decline in post-colonial Ghanaian society. The novel is a powerful critique of the disillusionment that followed independence, as the hopes for a better future were replaced by greed and the loss of morality.

The novel vividly portrays the widespread corruption in the country, where political and social systems are tainted by avarice and opportunism. The man's refusal to partake in corrupt practices sets him apart in a society where such behaviour is normalized. His commitment to integrity isolates him from his peers, family and society, highlighting the personal cost of maintaining moral standards in a corrupt world. Armah thus contrasts the pursuit of material wealth with the value of personal integrity. The man's rejection of 'the gleam' – a symbol of material success – underscores the emptiness of such pursuits when achieved through unethical means.

The Beautyful Ones Are Not Yet Born challenges readers to reflect on their own values and the society that shapes them. It suggests that while moral integrity may come with significant personal sacrifice, it is a vital and courageous stance against corruption and decay. The title itself, drawn from a hopeful inscription on a bus, implies that true beauty and goodness – embodied in integrity – may still emerge in the future, even if they are not yet visible in the present. Armah's work serves as both a lament for a society's moral failures and a call to uphold personal honour in the face of overwhelming odds.

Alternative Remedy:
For a satirical and darkly funny take on post-colonial corruption try *Wizard of the Crow* (2006) by Kenyan writer and academic Ngũgĩ wa Thiong'o.

CONDITION OR SITUATION:
Maintaining Dignity in the Face of Adversity

PRESCRIPTION:
One Day in the Life of Ivan Denisovich (1962)
by Aleksandr Solzhenitsyn

'That bowl of soup – it was dearer than freedom, dearer than life itself, past, present and future.'

Aleksandr Solzhenitsyn's short but powerful novel records a single day in the life of Ivan Denisovich Shukhov, a Soviet labour camp prisoner during the 1950s.

As in Herta Müller's *The Hunger Angel*, Solzhenitsyn's story details the brutality and dehumanization experienced by inmates at the camp, where they are forced to work in extreme cold, with little food and shelter, and are subjected to random acts of humiliation and violence.

However, Solzhenitsyn shares with the reader the ways and means the prisoners adopt to try to retain their dignity and purpose in life. He shows how individuals can adapt to even the most extreme situations and cope with the psychological strain and trauma inflicted upon them.

By small acts of resistance and defiance, however simple, such as hiding a piece of bread, or stopping work to watch the beauty of a sunrise, Ivan asserts his sense of dignity despite the oppression he is experiencing. Solzhenitsyn (who himself spent eight years in one of Stalin's gulags) argues that even in the most difficult of circumstances, strength, joy and meaning can be derived from things as simple as a good conversation, a warm meal or observing something of beauty.

The novel also highlights the importance, to all of us, of solidarity and community. Ivan and his fellow prisoners share a sense of camaraderie and form an understanding between themselves which helps them to cope with the cruelty of their situation.

In short, despite the uttermost suffering and indignities experienced by Ivan and his fellow inmates, Solzhenitsyn shows the reader, in this snapshot of life in a Soviet labour camp, that even in these bleak and extreme conditions individuals can maintain their humanity, dignity and purpose.

Alternative Remedy:

For another dose of dignity and resilience in the face of hardship and cruelty try *Papillon* (1969) by Henri Charrière, the purportedly true story of a man wrongfully convicted of murder and incarcerated on the notorious penal colony of Devil's Island in French Guiana.

CONDITION OR SITUATION:
Fighting the Patriarchy and Building Resistance

PRESCRIPTION:
The Handmaid's Tale (1985)
by Margaret Atwood

'There is no such thing as a sterile man anymore, not officially. There are only women who are fruitful and women who are barren, that's the law.'

This dystopian novel explores a patriarchal, fundamentalist society where women have lost all their rights and are forced into reproductive servitude. It is a scathing critique of societies that oppress and marginalize women.

Set in the near future, the story follows Offred, a 'Handmaid' who is assigned to produce children for a powerful Commander and his barren wife, Serena Joy, in the fictitious Republic of Gilead. Gilead's regime is an extreme example of a society that values male power and control over women's bodies and lives.

By highlighting the complex power dynamics between different groups in Gilead, including the Commanders, the Wives, the Handmaids and the Econowives, the novel examines how power is exercised and maintained through a system of oppression and control.

The Handmaid's Tale also explores the importance of memory and history in shaping our understanding of the present and future. Offred's memories of her past life and her daughter serve as a reminder of what has been lost and what is worth fighting for. Her story is a testament to the human spirit's ability to resist and survive in the face of oppression, and the novel shows how women find ways to subvert the system, resist their oppressors, and maintain their sense of self and identity.

This novel highlights the importance of women's reproductive rights and autonomy. It was inspired by Atwood's concern about the dangers to women's rights posed by the rise to prominence of right-wing religious fundamentalism in the US during the 1980s. The author has described her novel not as science fiction but as 'speculative fiction', the difference being the former describes something that predicts a possible future whereas the latter describes something that is possible in the known present, i.e. now.

Alternative Remedy:
Red Clocks (2018) by Leni Zumas is another novel about a not-too-distant version of America where all abortion is banned and women's reproductive rights are strictly controlled.

CONDITION OR SITUATION:
The Search for Freedom and Finding Oneself

PRESCRIPTION:
The Country Girls (1960)
by Edna O'Brien

*'But being myself never seemed impossible
or ludicrous or even that difficult.'*

The novel *The Country Girls* explores the lives of two young women, Caithleen and Baba, growing up in rural Ireland in the 1950s. It delves into themes of identity and self-discovery as the girls struggle to find their place in the world, manage their relationships, and define themselves amid the constraints of small-town life. *The Country Girls* is a coming-of-age novel that examines the challenges of leaving childhood behind, navigating adolescence, and entering adulthood, all set against the backdrop of a rapidly changing Ireland.

A major influence upon the girls' lives is their Catholic faith, including the guilt, shame and repression that accompany its strict moral code. The novel is a scathing critique of the patriarchal society that governs every aspect of women's lives, from their relationships to their reproductive rights. The girls' struggles to assert their independence, to make their own choices and to forge their own paths are constantly thwarted by the oppressive forces of family, church and community. Readers will gain insight into the ways in which societal norms and expectations can limit individual freedom and autonomy, particularly for women.

O'Brien highlights the significance of female relationships in facing the challenges of life, especially in patriarchal societies. The complex, often fraught, bond between Caithleen and Baba serves as a source of comfort, support and strength. Despite the challenges and hardships faced by the girls, their story ultimately offers a message of hope and resilience, highlighting the human capacity to adapt, survive and thrive in the face of adversity.

The Country Girls demonstrates the importance of self-awareness, self-acceptance and self-discovery in shaping one's identity and finding one's place in the world.

Alternative Remedies:

The Country Girls is the first part of a trilogy of novels – followed by *The Lonely Girl* (1962) and *Girls in Their Married Bliss* (1964) – which detail the further adventures of Caithleen and Baba. Fellow Irish writer Anne Enright's novel *The Wig My Father Wore* (1995) covers similar themes of love and self-discovery.

CONDITION OR SITUATION:
Building Up Resilience in the Face of Oppression

PRESCRIPTION:
The Color Purple (1982)
by Alice Walker

*'No person is your friend who demands your
silence, or denies your right to grow.'*

Many people feel that the odds are stacked against them, that life has dealt them a dud hand and that they are powerless and oppressed. If in need of some inspiration protein to build up resilience against the patriarchy, Alice Walker provides a healthy supplement. *The Color Purple* is a novel that explores the experiences of African–American women in the early twentieth century. The story follows Celie, a poor, uneducated black woman living in the rural South, as she navigates a life of poverty, abuse and marginalization.

The novel highlights the importance of female relationships and the ways in which women can support and empower each other. Celie's relationships with her sister Nettie, her friend Sofia and her lover Shug are central to the story. Walker explores the intersection of racism and sexism, demonstrating how these forms of oppression can be particularly devastating for African-American women. Celie faces both of these prejudices, which limit her opportunities and threaten her well-being. Her story is one of self-discovery, as she learns to value herself, her body and her experiences.

The Color Purple celebrates the importance of self-love and self-acceptance, particularly for women who have been marginalized and oppressed. The novel suggests that education is a key factor in empowering individuals, particularly women, as Celie's acquisition of literacy and her growing self-awareness enable her to challenge the patriarchal norms that have oppressed her. The novel celebrates the strength and resilience of women, particularly in the face of adversity, and highlights the importance of female empowerment and independence.

Alternative Remedy:
For another inspirational tale about overcoming oppression through the power of education try Nigerian-born writer Abi Daré's *The Girl with the Louding Voice* (2020).

CONDITION OR SITUATION:
Seeking Self-Confidence and Independence

PRESCRIPTION:
Jane Eyre (1846)
by Charlotte Brontë

'I can live alone, if self-respect, and circumstances require me so to do. I need not sell my soul to buy bliss.'

If I could go back and tweak the parenting of my daughter, one thing I would pay more attention to would be to try and nurture in her a love of classic literature. *Jane Eyre* is a book that every young girl should read. The novel is the quintessential nineteenth-century gothic romance, replete with forbidding grotesques and featuring austere settings concealing dark secrets. The story also examines the complexities of love and relationships, particularly in the context of Jane's tumultuous relationship with Mr Rochester.

The book explores Jane's struggles to define her own identity and morality, as she grapples with the conflicting demands of her conscience, her heart and her social circumstances. Jane's love of learning and her determination to educate herself demonstrate the transformative power of education and personal growth. Her journey shows the importance of valuing one's own autonomy and self-respect, even in the face of adversity or opposition. *Jane Eyre* also demonstrates the importance of emotional intelligence and empathy in building strong, healthy relationships and navigating complex social situations.

Although the issue of gender equality is not implicitly confronted, the novel nevertheless is considered to be an early proto-feminist book due to its depiction of the strong-willed central character who is resilient and resourceful, and takes on the Victorian patriarchy.

> **Alternative Remedy:**
> For an original re-imagining of the nineteenth-century gothic romance, try *Jane Steele* (2016) by American fantasy/crime writer Lyndsay Faye, which reworks the figure of Jane Eyre as a cheerful and plucky serial killer.

MEDICINE CABINET ESSENTIALS:
Adventures of Huckleberry Finn (1884)
by Mark Twain

This classic American novel follows the journey of Huck Finn, a young boy who runs away from his abusive father, Pap, and embarks on a rafting adventure down the Mississippi River with Jim, a runaway slave. As they travel, Huck and Jim face various challenges and moral dilemmas, encountering a range of characters from con artists and thieves to feuding families and kind-hearted philanthropists. Throughout their journey, Huck learns valuable lessons about loyalty, compassion and the complexities of human nature.

Huck's journey is a classic coming-of-age story, as he navigates the challenges of adulthood, contending with moral dilemmas and learning to make decisions based on his own developing values. The novel explores the morally reprehensible institution of slavery and the racist attitudes that perpetuated it. Through Huck's relationship with Jim, Twain criticizes the society of the time, stressing the humanity and dignity of enslaved people.

The bond between Huck and Jim demonstrates the transformative power of friendship and loyalty, showing that

strong relationships can overcome even the most daunting challenges. The novel teaches the importance of treating others with kindness and understanding, regardless of their background or circumstances.

One central theme of the book is personal freedom, with Twain particularly critical of the so-called 'sivilising' (sic) attitudes of the 'Old South', with its prejudices, materialism and moral corruption. Huck and Jim's journey down the river becomes a metaphor for a journey of self-discovery and freedom through communion with the natural world away from the stifling pressures of society.

> *'Right is right, and wrong is wrong, and a*
> *body ain't got no business doing wrong when*
> *he ain't ignorant and knows better.'*

CONDITION OR SITUATION:
Understanding Moral Duties

PRESCRIPTION:
Schindler's List (1982)
by Thomas Keneally

'Whoever saves one life saves the entire world.'

Originally published as *Schindler's Ark,* this novel sends a powerful message to the reader about understanding moral obligations and doing the right thing, as well as the tragic consequences of choosing not to.

Set between 1939 and 1945 during the Nazi occupation of Poland, the book tells of industrialist Oskar Schindler's growing sense of compassion for the Jews he employs in his factory, and his determination to try to save as many of them as possible from the Nazi death camps despite considerable danger to himself.

It takes Schindler a great deal of courage and resourcefulness, risking his own life and livelihood, in order to stand by his own moral compass. The reader is shown how much impact his actions had on those he helped, proving that compassion and empathy are crucial and are the basis of our moral obligations to ourselves and others.

The novel shows that an individual can have a significant effect on the lives of others and it is one's moral duty to muster the courage to do this, even in the face of oppression or indifference. Keneally warns the reader of the devastating consequences of doing nothing, exemplified by the fate of Jews under the Nazi regime.

Schindler's List gives the reader a thought-provoking study of the complexities of human nature, and of human morality put to the ultimate test.

Alternative Remedy:
For an alternative take on the traumas of the Holocaust and its lasting legacy on survivors' lives, try *Maus* (1991) by Art Spiegelman, the only graphic novel to be awarded the Pulitzer Prize.

CONDITION OR SITUATION:
Issues with Self-Fulfilment

PRESCRIPTION:
Their Eyes Were Watching God (1937)
by Zora Neale Hurston

'They sat in company with the others in other shanties, their eyes straining against crude walls and their souls asking if He meant to measure their puny might against His. They seemed to be staring at the dark, but their eyes were watching God.'

An example of classic African-American literature, *Their Eyes Were Watching God* follows the life of the central character, Janie Crawford, in the early twentieth century. It explores her journey towards self-discovery, independence and self-fulfilment, as she faces the expectations placed on her as an African-American woman in the American South.

Through her journey, the novel foregrounds the importance of self-acceptance and learning to love oneself. Janie gains an appreciation of her own strengths, weaknesses and individuality, enabling her to finally reject the negative self-image that has been thrust upon her by society.

A key aspect in her story is Janie's desire for independence and the right to be allowed to make her own decisions about her life. She finds that she must have this autonomy in order to achieve true self-realization. Hurston emphasizes how important personal growth is to all of us by chronicling Janie's navigation of the challenges and complexities of life, demonstrating that self-fulfilment is not a static state, rather it is an ongoing process of growth and development.

Through Janie's love of nature and appreciation of beauty, along with her need to tell her own story, the novel teaches the reader the need for self-expression and creativity. This personal journey is entwined with her growing sense of connection to her community, her heritage and her culture, demonstrating that a person's own goals and aspirations are often determined by the well-being of others.

Their Eyes Were Watching God provides readers with a broad exploration of self-fulfilment and an understanding of what it means to achieve it. The novel focuses our attention on the themes of self-discovery, voice, autonomy and nature, and employs them to highlight the importance of achieving a fulfilling life through self-love, self-acceptance and self-expression.

Alternative Remedy:
The Vanishing Half (2020) by Brit Bennett covers similar themes of finding self-fulfilment as it tells the story of two identical twins' traumatic childhood.

CONDITION OR SITUATION:
Throwing Off the Shackles of Social Conformity

PRESCRIPTION:
The Age of Innocence (1920)
by Edith Wharton

'With a shiver of foreboding he saw his marriage becoming what most of the other marriages about him were: a dull association of material and social interests held together by ignorance on the one side and hypocrisy on the other.'

Edith Wharton's *The Age of Innocence* explores the complexities of nineteenth-century New York high society through the story of Newland Archer, a wealthy lawyer who becomes engaged to May Welland but finds himself drawn to her cousin, the exotic and independent Countess Ellen Olenska. Torn between his desire for Ellen and his obligation to May, Archer is aware that pursuing a relationship with Ellen would be considered scandalous and would likely damage his reputation and social standing. Through Newland Archer's inner conflict, Wharton questions whether it is better to conform to societal duty or to follow one's own desires and aspirations.

Through this tension, the novel vividly portrays the rigid

social conventions and expectations that govern the lives of New York's elite. Wharton also critiques the excesses and superficiality of the Gilded Age society, highlighting the ways in which social status and material comfort can stifle individuality and genuine human connection. At the centre is a clash between old-fashioned values and traditions, and the more progressive attitudes of the early twentieth century. The emerging modernity is embodied by characters like Countess Olenska, who represents a more liberated and independent way of living.

Newland Archer's conflict illustrates the challenges of breaking free from the expectations of society. However, despite the social constraints, the message of *The Age of Innocence* is that individuals can achieve a measure of inner freedom by cultivating their own thoughts, feelings and desires. Archer's turmoil and his emotional connection with Ellen represent a form of this freedom, even if he is unable to fully express it in his outward life.

Alternative Remedy:
For an alternative exploration of the tensions between the old-fashioned world and the new try *The Portrait of a Lady* (1881) by Henry James.

5

Remedies for Everyday Living

CONDITION OR SITUATION:
Fear of the Future

PRESCRIPTION:
Last Love in Constantinople (1994)
by Milorad Pavić

'I knew I should not touch the living with the same hand that had touched the dead in my dreams.'

Although at least two thirds of my own life has passed, I can empathize with people who suffer from anxiety about what the future may bring, especially amid today's global uncertainties and the withering speed of change. A postmodern, experimental work that defies traditional narrative structures, *Last Love in Constantinople* addresses such fears of the future.

The story is set in seventeenth-century Constantinople (modern-day Istanbul) and follows a series of characters, including a young nobleman, a beautiful woman and a mysterious tarot card reader. The plot revolves around the search for a lost love, a mysterious manuscript and a series of cryptic messages and prophecies.

The work is presented as a 'tarot novel', with each chapter corresponding to a specific tarot card. The narrative is non-linear, and the characters' stories are intertwined and overlapping. The tarot cards serve as a symbol of fate and destiny, which can be seen as a force beyond human control. The characters' lives are shaped by the cards, which implies that their futures are predetermined. This can be seen as a reflection of the human fear of being at the mercy of forces beyond our control, and the anxiety that comes with not being able to shape our own destinies.

The novel's non-linear narrative structure and use of tarot cards blur the boundaries between time and perception. This creates a sense of timelessness, where the past, present and future are intertwined. This blurring of boundaries can evoke fears about the future, as it suggests that our actions in the present may have unforeseen consequences in the future, and that the past can continue to shape our lives in ways we cannot fully understand.

> **Alternative Remedy:**
> For anyone anxious about the future, try *Blindness* (1995) by Portuguese Nobel Prize-winner José Saramago. This is a truly terrifying metaphorical parable of society disintegrating with withering speed after a mysterious pandemic.

MEDICINE CABINET ESSENTIALS:

The Diary of a Young Girl (1947)
by Anne Frank

This book is the actual diary written by Anne Frank, a young Jewish girl living in Nazi-occupied Amsterdam during World War II. It documents her day-to-day life from June 1942 until August 1944.

Commencing on her thirteenth birthday, after receiving a blank diary as a gift, Anne writes about her life, her interactions with family and friends, and her dreams and expectations about her future. However, to try to avoid capture by the Nazis, her family are forced to hide, along with four others, in a cramped annex above her father's office building. Despite this, she continues to keep her diary, recording the daily difficulties and terror that she feels, but still telling of her hopes and dreams, finding beauty in little things in life.

As a primary source document, *The Diary of a Young Girl* furnishes the reader with an understanding of the actual experiences of those who lived during World War II, and helps to develop empathy for victims of not only the Holocaust, but also of all other genocides.

Anne inspires the reader through the courage, resilience and optimism she shows in a time of overwhelming adversity and danger, and the book teaches that even in the darkest of times, with hope and spirit people can summon the courage to try to survive. The diary conveys a message of hope and compassion, as well as the importance of protecting everyone's human rights. Anne shows us the value of tolerance and to appreciate the worth and dignity of the individual.

Everyone should read this account of ordinary people facing discrimination, prejudice and genocide, as unfortunately disregard for human rights continues today in many parts of the world. Sadly, lessons still have to be learned from the atrocity of the Holocaust.

> *'It's difficult in times like these: ideals, dreams and cherished hopes rise within us, only to be crushed by grim reality. It's a wonder I haven't abandoned all my ideals, they seem so absurd and impractical. Yet I cling to them because I still believe, in spite of everything, that people are truly good at heart.'*

CONDITION OR SITUATION:
Recovering From a Long Illness

PRESCRIPTION:
The Magic Mountain (1924)
by Thomas Mann

'The human soul is a restless traveller, forever seeking fulfilment in the promise of the future.'

Should one be laid up for any notable period of time, either recovering from a major operation, recuperating from illness, or bedridden with the flu, try reading the ultimate in 'sick lit'. The narrative of *The Magic Mountain* takes place at a sanatorium in the Swiss Alps where the protagonist, Hans Castorp, visits his cousin and becomes embroiled in a world of intellectual and philosophical debates.

The Magic Mountain is set in the years leading up to World War I, and Mann is critical of the social, cultural and intellectual trends that contributed to the war. The novel portrays a Europe in decline, where traditional values and institutions are crumbling, and new, more radical ideologies are emerging. As Hans navigates the complex and often contradictory world of the sanatorium, he must confront his own values, beliefs and sense of purpose. There is a tension and conflict between rationality and passion as embodied in the characters of Settembrini, an Italian humanist intellectual and Clavdia, a mysterious and alluring woman who represents unchained emotion and intuition.

Mann explores the theme of illness and suffering as a catalyst for personal growth and transformation. Hans' experiences at the sanatorium, where he is surrounded by people suffering from tuberculosis, force him to confront his own mortality and the fragility of human life. Illness is represented as much as of the mind as of the body (in fact it is never entirely clear if Hans is actually sick).

The novel celebrates the power of art and imagination to transcend the limitations of human experience and to provide a deeper understanding of the world. Mann draws on a wide range of cultural and intellectual references, from music and literature to philosophy and psychology, to create a rich and complex portrait of human existence.

Alternative Remedy:

For a more contemporary examination of illness as a metaphor for personal growth try *The Fault in Our Stars* (2012) by John Green, a heartbreaking love story about two teenagers with terminal cancer.

CONDITION OR SITUATION:
Understanding the Power of Communities

PRESCRIPTION:
The Bridge on the Drina (1945)
by Ivo Andrić

'Life flows on, people come and go, but the bridge remains. A bridge is not just a connection between two places, but a symbol of unity and strength.'

The Serbian–Croatian former diplomat Ivo Andrić has written here a love letter to a bridge, the people who built it, used it and lived around it, and how their lives were shaped by the bridge's presence through the centuries. The story of the bridge begins with its construction during the Ottoman Empire in the sixteenth century and the book follows its history right up to its fate during World War I when it was partially destroyed. Although the book looks at historical events, its non-linear narrative and multiple perspectives show how different people can have different experiences and understandings of the same event or place.

In the Balkans, several cultures, religions and empires have intersected, influenced and conflicted with one another over the centuries. The bridge itself represents the connections between different people and communities, illustrating the ways in which our lives are intertwined and also interdependent. As a symbol of these links, the bridge emphasizes the importance of building and maintaining relationships with others – metaphorically building bridges. The novel also explores the complexities of national identity, particularly in the context of the many different groups that met in the Balkans.

The Bridge on the Drina is a testament to the power of storytelling, showing how stories can be used to connect us to our past, our culture and each other.

> **Alternative Remedy:**
> For a contemporary slice of Balkan fiction examining the impact of conflict on communities, try *The Cellist of Sarajevo* (2008) by Steven Galloway, set during the Bosnian War of the 1990s and partly based on a true story.

CONDITION OR SITUATION:
Managing Life Expectations

PRESCRIPTION:
American Pastoral (1997)
by Philip Roth

'There was a big belief in life and we were steered relentlessly in the direction of success: a better existence was going to be ours. The goal was to have goals, the aim to have aims.'

Perhaps we are led to believe that we are entitled to more from life than we actually receive? The American Dream states that anyone can live a prosperous life through hard work, determination and quality of opportunity, but could this lead to unrealistic expectations?

American Pastoral explores the American Dream, disillusionment, and the myth of social mobility. It is also an intricate examination of identity, family and the tensions between reality and expectation.

The book is narrated by Nathan Zuckerman (an alter ego of Roth), a writer and observer of the human condition, who reflects on the story of his high school classmate, Seymour 'the Swede' Levov. The Swede's idyllic life is turned upside down when his daughter, Merry, becomes involved in radical politics and commits a violent act, setting off a disastrous chain of events.

The novel portrays the complex and often fraught relationships within families, particularly between parents and children. The relationship between the Swede and Merry is an example of this, as the Swede struggles to understand and connect with his daughter, her motivations and who she really is. Roth also explores the tension and fragmentation between different identities and the difficulties of maintaining a coherent sense of self: the Swede is torn between his Jewish heritage and his desire to assimilate into American society.

American Pastoral is a novel that offers insights into the challenges of managing life expectations. It serves as a reminder that life is complex and often unpredictable, and there are many ways in which it can be disrupted by unexpected events or circumstances. Ultimately, *American Pastoral* suggests that the American Dream is a myth, an unattainable ideal that can lead to disillusionment and discontent, and that we are all just one poor decision away from a fall from grace.

Alternative Remedy:
Vineland (1990) by Thomas Pynchon also explores themes of loss of ideals and the hollowness of contemporary American culture.

CONDITION OR SITUATION:
Dealing with Bureaucracy

PRESCRIPTION:
The Trial (1925)
by Franz Kafka

'Logic is no doubt unshakable, but it can't withstand a person who wants to live. Where was the judge he'd never seen? Where was the high court he'd never reached?'

Ever have those days where you feel like sticking your fingers in your ears and letting out a long, anguished scream at the world? Being kept endlessly on hold while mind-numbing elevator music repeats over and over in your head; being bounced from department to department like the shuttlecock in a seemingly eternal game of bureaucratic badminton until to your horror you find yourself back where you started? Czech writer Franz Kafka was so adroit at expressing this peculiar sense of existential desolation caused by institutional bureaucracy that his works spawned their own adjective: Kafkaesque.

The Trial, published posthumously in 1925, is Kafka's masterpiece – a coruscating parable of the nightmarish effects of faceless bureaucracy. The story follows the protagonist,

Josef K, a lowly bank official who is arrested and put on trial without knowing the charges against him. Throughout the novel, Josef K. searches for answers and tries to understand the nature of the trial and what crime he is accused of, but is thwarted by a series of often contradictory or impossible tests and challenges that keep him from discovering the truth.

Josef K.'s experience is a powerful exploration of the alienating effects of modern society, where individuals are reduced to mere cogs in a machine and are unable to connect with others or find meaning in their lives. In particular, *The Trial* is a scathing critique of the dehumanizing effects of bureaucracy, highlighting the ways in which individuals can become trapped in a labyrinthine system that is seemingly designed to confuse and oppress.

The Trial offers readers a profound and unsettling exploration of the human condition and a potent warning about the dangers of unchecked bureaucratic power. In this book, Kafka stresses the importance of individual autonomy and agency.

Alternative Remedies:
The works of British novelist Magnus Mills, author of *The Restraint of Beasts* (1998) and *The Scheme for Full Employment* (2003), are often compared to Franz Kafka in their unsettling depiction of seemingly mundane situations as sinister, oppressive and not what they seem.

CONDITION OR SITUATION:
Working through Family Expectations

PRESCRIPTION:
A Suitable Boy (1993)
by Vikram Seth

'Sometimes, the most beautiful things in life are the simplest ones – a smile, a touch, a kind word.'

It is not uncommon to find oneself caught in the dichotomy between what one 'should do' and what one 'could do'. This dilemma is often exacerbated by family or societal/cultural pressures. *A Suitable Boy* is set in post-independence India and revolves around the life of Lata, a young woman from a middle-class family, as she confronts the intricacies of love, family, and cultural and historical expectations. Her story sheds light on the difficulties of assuaging family obligations while staying true to one's own desires and aspirations.

One of the primary concerns of the novel is the pressure exerted by families on their children in matters of marriage and career. Lata's mother, Mrs Rupa Mehra, is determined to find a suitable husband for her daughter, and the novel delves into the intricacies of arranged marriages and the compromises that often come with them.

Lata's journey is marked by her struggle to reconcile her own wishes with the assumptions of her family, particularly her mother's. The novel also highlights the importance of communication and openness in managing family pressures. Lata's relationships with her family members are tangled and difficult, and the novel demonstrates how open and honest communication can help to alleviate some of the tensions that arise from conflicting ideals. Through its exploration of the tricky webs within families and the tension between tradition and modernity, *A Suitable Boy* provides a vivid portrayal of the difficulties faced by individuals in balancing the complexities of family expectations.

Alternative Remedy:
Clear Light of Day (1980) by Anita Desai explores families, marriage and the role of women in a rapidly changing Indian society.

CONDITION OR SITUATION:
Wanting to Live Life to the Full

PRESCRIPTION:
Zorba the Greek (1946)
by Nikos Kazantzakis

'How simple and frugal a thing is happiness: a glass of wine, a roast chestnut, a wretched little brazier, the sound of the sea. Nothing else. And all that is required to feel that here and now is happiness is a simple, frugal heart.'

The overarching message in *Zorba the Greek* is the importance of living life to the full. Based on Nikos Kazantzakis' own experiences on the island of Crete, the story explores the relationship between a young, intellectual Greek man, 'the Boss', and a local character, Alexis Zorba. Zorba is a vibrant and engaging free spirit who lives in the moment and who takes on the joys and challenges of life with energy and passion. The two men spend many hours together, during which Zorba passes on his wisdom to the Boss on how to live life to the full.

The Boss and Zorba are from totally different backgrounds, and the novel puts forward to the reader the ways in which life experience and instinctive knowledge contrast with intellectual endeavour. The relationship between the two individuals exemplifies the ways in which friendships and connections can help us to learn from each other, see things from different perspectives, and challenge our assumptions about life. The intellect of the Boss and his initial struggle to find meaning in life is balanced with Zorba's philosophy of living in the present moment and a refusal to get hung up with worries about the past or future.

Within *Zorba the Greek* is the message that we should approach life with a sense of wonder, curiosity and enthusiasm, and that we have the option to pick how we live our lives, creating our meaning and purpose even when facing uncertainty and hardship. Kazantzakis encourages us to be unafraid to follow our hearts and to trust our instincts, and to follow Zorba's take on life, which embraces a willingness to take risks, go with the flow, and not try to control or foresee the outcome of future events.

Alternative Remedy:
Another novel that encourages readers to live life to the full and has a similar enchanted feeling is *One Hundred Years of Solitude* (1967) by Gabriel Garcia Márquez.

MEDICINE CABINET ESSENTIALS:
Little Women (1868–69)
by Louisa May Alcott

This coming-of-age novel follows the lives of the four March sisters – Meg, Jo, Beth and Amy – as they face the challenges of adolescence and young adulthood during the American Civil War era. The story is loosely based on Alcott's own experiences growing up with her three sisters.

As the story unfolds, the sisters experience love, loss and personal growth, all while learning valuable lessons about family, friendship and the importance of staying true to oneself. Jo, the protagonist, is a strong-willed and independent young woman who dreams of becoming a writer, while Meg, the beautiful and responsible older sister, endures the complexities of romance and social expectations. Beth, the shy and gentle sister, faces a life-threatening illness, and Amy, the artistic and spoiled youngest girl, learns to balance her creative ambitions with the demands of growing up. *Little Women* explores the challenges and triumphs of leaving childhood behind, as the sisters explore and develop their own personalities, ambitions and relationships.

Louisa May Alcott's timeless classic celebrates the bonds of family and sisterhood, highlighting the importance of female relationships and the support women provide to each other.

The story also embodies and promotes the importance of universal values such as honesty, kindness and generosity, as the sisters face various moral dilemmas and learn and grow from their experiences.

'Far away there in the sunshine are my highest aspirations. I may not reach them, but I can look up and see their beauty, believe in them, and try to follow where they lead.'

CONDITION OR SITUATION:
Issues with Families and Social Obligations

PRESCRIPTION:
The God of Small Things (1997)
by Arundhati Roy

'And the air was full of Thoughts and Things to Say. But at times like these, only the Small Things are ever said. Big Things lurk unsaid inside.'

Arundhati Roy's Booker Prize-winning novel *The God of Small Things* revolves around the lives of the twins Rahel and Estha, and their experiences growing up in Kerala, India, in the 1960s. Through their story, Roy examines the lasting impact of traumatic events on individuals and families. The twins' experiences, particularly the tragic death of their cousin Sophie Mol, shape their lives and relationships, demonstrating how memories can be both a source of pain and a means of healing.

The novel delves into the tensions between traditional Indian culture and modernity, as well as the struggles of individuals to find their place within these conflicting worlds.

Roy's characters grapple with questions of identity, cultural heritage and belonging, reflecting the trials faced by many people in a rapidly changing world.

At the centre of the narrative lies an exploration of the complexities of human relationships, in particular within the family, and the book looks at the ways in which love, loyalty and betrayal can intersect and influence one another. Roy suggests that it is these intricate webs that bind family members together. Through the characters' experiences, readers gain insight into the ways in which family dynamics can shape our identities and worldviews.

The characters' struggles with trauma and guilt also show readers the importance of forgiveness, not just for others, but also for oneself, and the role it plays in moving on from stifling and oppressive life issues.

Finally, *The God of Small Things* critiques the rigid social hierarchy and caste system in India, exposing the injustices and cruelties that arise from these systems. Roy sheds light on the struggles of the marginalized and the oppressed, encouraging us to question and challenge these social norms.

Alternative Remedy:
For a different angle on the Asian caste system with a modern setting try *Moth Smoke* (2000) by British Pakistani writer Mohsin Hamid.

CONDITION OR SITUATION:
Embracing Spontaneity and Living for the Moment

PRESCRIPTION:
On the Road (1957)
by Jack Kerouac

'My whole wretched life swam before my weary eyes, and I realized no matter what you do it's bound to be a waste of time in the end so you might as well go mad.'

In certain circumstances it is wise to tread carefully; as Shakespeare's Falstaff famously observed: 'The better part of valour is discretion ...' (*Henry IV*, Part 1, Act 5, Scene 4). In general, however, being cautious is just a personality trait, and should you feel that life is passing you by and you need inspiration to *carpe diem*, seek out a copy of *On the Road*.

This novel explores themes of freedom, spontaneity and the search for meaning and identity. It follows the journey of Sal Paradise, a young writer, and his friend Dean Moriarty, a charismatic and energetic free spirit, as they travel across the United States in the late 1940s. The book is a semi-autobiographical account of Kerouac's own experiences with his friends, including fellow writer Neal Cassady, who inspired the character of Dean Moriarty. The story is a celebration of the open road, the beauty of the American landscape, and the freedom to explore and experience new things.

The novel emphasizes the importance of living in the present moment, and of being fully engaged with the world around us. The characters are constantly seeking new experiences, and are willing to take risks and challenge themselves in order to live life to the fullest. *On the Road* teaches us that life is a journey, not a destination, and that the experiences and encounters we have along the way are what give life its meaning and significance.

Alternative Remedy:
For an extreme account of throwing caution to the wind, try *Tap Dancing on Everest* (2024) by Mimi Zieman, the true story of an expedition to climb the perilous east face of the Himalayan mountain without the use of oxygen.

CONDITION OR SITUATION:
Adapting to a Changing World

PRESCRIPTION:
Things Fall Apart (1958)
by Chinua Achebe

'The drums were still beating, persistent and unchanging. Their sound was no longer a separate thing from the living village. It was like the pulsation of its heart.'

Change can be a daunting prospect for people to adapt to. There is a sense that traditions uphold certain values and reinforce a way of life. Sudden upheavals can be traumatic and life-altering. *Things Fall Apart* by Nigerian author Chinua Achebe tells the story of Okonkwo, a respected warrior of the Igbo tribe, and his struggles with the changing world around him. The novel explores the rich cultural heritage of the Igbo people, highlighting the importance of tradition, customs and values in shaping personal and communal identity. Achebe critiques the destructive impact of British colonialism on Igbo society, revealing the ways in which foreign powers can disrupt and erode traditional cultures.

Okonkwo's character embodies the traditional Igbo ideals of masculinity, which are challenged by the changing social and cultural landscape. Through his story, Achebe explores the tension between individual desires and communal expectations, highlighting the importance of balancing personal aspirations with social responsibilities. By showing how the characters respond to the rapid changes brought about by colonialism, the book emphasizes the need for adaptability and resilience in the face of uncertainty.

Things Fall Apart provides a unique window into the culture, traditions and history of the Igbo people, offering insights into the complexities of an African society. The novel encourages readers to think critically about the consequences of rapid change and the importance of preserving cultural heritage in the face of modernization.

Alternative Remedy:
Ghanaian-American writer Yaa Gyasi's historical epic *Homegoing* (2016) touches on similar areas, such as the effect of colonialism on communities and families.

CONDITION OR SITUATION:
Coping with Jealousy and Envy

PRESCRIPTION:
The Blue Umbrella (1980)
by Ruskin Bond

*'The umbrella was like a flower, a great blue flower
that had sprung up on the dry brown hillside.'*

Part of the Tenth Commandment in the Bible addresses the sin of covetousness and quite explicitly forbids envy and desiring another's possessions. In no particular order, your neighbour's house, wife, oxen and servants are specifically mentioned. But what if the object of jealousy is a handsome blue umbrella?

The Blue Umbrella is a novella by Indian writer Ruskin Bond about a young girl named Binya, who lives in a small village in the Himalayas. Binya is a carefree and simple girl who owns a rare object, a beautiful blue umbrella, a gift from a foreign tourist. The umbrella becomes the centre of attention in the village, and soon, the shopkeeper, Ram Bharose, becomes obsessed with acquiring it.

As the story unfolds, Ram Bharose's jealousy of Binya grows, and he tries various ways to obtain the blue umbrella from her. However, Binya is not willing to part with her beloved umbrella.

Binya's cheerful and simple nature is contrasted with Ram Bharose's growing dissatisfaction and envy, highlighting the importance of being content with what one has. Her innocence and naïvety are portrayed as a source of strength, allowing her to remain unaffected by Ram Bharose's machinations.

The Blue Umbrella is a gentle parable showing that jealousy and envy can be destructive emotions that can consume a person's life. Ram Bharose's character serves as a warning about the dangers of allowing these emotions to take over, as it leads to a loss of integrity, relationships and, ultimately, his well-being. Through Binya's character, the novella shows that true happiness and serenity come from within and that simplicity and innocence can be powerful antidotes to the corrosive effects of envy. It encourages us to reflect on the importance of gratitude and contentment, and the dangers of allowing negative emotions to dominate our lives.

Alternative Remedy:
Wise and Otherwise: A Salute to Life (2002) by best-selling Indian author Sudha Murty is a charming collection of fifty vignettes or snapshots of human stories of greed, jealousy, generosity and selflessness.

CONDITION OR SITUATION:
Overcoming the Superficiality of Middle-Class Values

PRESCRIPTION:
I Am a Cat (1906)
by Natsume Sōseki

'Let all mankind remember in what self-complacent idleness they used to pass their days; how passionately they once believed that impassivity of mind and body were the signs of a noble soul.'

This novel, set in early twentieth-century Japan, follows the lives of a middle-class family through the eyes of an unnamed cat, whose commentary on the social norms of the time is both satirical and humorous, exposing superficiality and contradictions in the humans he observes.

The cat is ideally placed to ridicule the hypocrisy of the human family members. Modernization and Westernization were having an effect on Japanese life at this time and the cat is able to observe how these social and cultural changes were impacting the family on a day-to-day basis. There are obvious tensions between differing social classes, and the humans struggle to maintain an air of respectability in order to retain their middle-class position on the social ladder, despite their flaws and weaknesses which float beneath the surface. Their lives are governed by empty conventions and societal rules, leading to an affected and pretentious etiquette.

Through the eyes of the cat, Sōseki cleverly examines the human condition. The novel provides the reader with a thoughtful commentary on the way social pressures structure our behaviour and affect how we interact with others. It suggests that authenticity is hard to find in a society ruled by superficial values. By studying the themes and message in this novel, *I Am a Cat* allows us to attain a deeper understanding of the underlying complexities of human nature and the often seemingly shallow social conventions by which we are ruled.

Alternative Remedy:
The Life of Insects (1993) by Russian writer Victor Pelevin explores a society facing sudden change and draws allegorical comparisons between Russian society adapting to the fall of communism with the parallel lives of various mosquitoes, cockroaches and other insects.

MEDICINE CABINET ESSENTIALS:
Don Quixote (1605)
by Miguel de Cervantes

More commonly known as *Dox Quixote*, *The Ingenious Gentleman Don Quixote of La Mancha*, by Miguel de Cervantes, is widely regarded as one of the first novels and a cornerstone of Western literature. Set in early seventeenth-century Spain, the story follows Alonso Quixano, a middle-aged gentleman from La Mancha who, after reading countless chivalric romances, loses touch with reality and decides to become a knight-errant under the name Don Quixote. Convinced he must revive the age of chivalry, he dons rusty armour, mounts his old horse Rocinante, and sets out on a series of misguided adventures to right wrongs and defend the helpless.

Accompanied by his loyal squire, Sancho Panza – a pragmatic, earthy peasant who provides a grounded counterpoint to Don Quixote's idealism – the 'Knight of the Woeful Countenance' encounters windmills he mistakes for giants, innkeepers he believes to be lords, and various characters who often exploit or mock his delusions. The novel blends slapstick humour, satire and profound human insight, exploring the clash between fantasy and reality, and culminating in a poignant reflection on identity, purpose and mortality.

Don Quixote's apparent insanity – his inability to distinguish fiction from fact – raises deeper questions about perception and truth. Cervantes suggests that what society deems 'mad' may carry a kind of wisdom, as Don Quixote's delusions often reveal the noblest of intentions.

Cervantes uses Don Quixote's misadventures to satirize the rigid class structures, outdated traditions and hypocrisy of Spanish society at the time. The novel critiques the decline of chivalric ideals and the materialism that replaced them.

Don Quixote's unrelenting pursuit of his ideals, however delusional, serves as a powerful reminder of the importance of dreams and imagination. In a world often dulled by routine and cynicism, his story encourages us to envision a better reality and to pursue our passions, no matter how improbable they seem, by reigniting a sense of wonder and possibility.

> *'The truth may be stretched thin, but it never breaks,*
> *and it always surfaces above lies, as oil floats on water.'*

CONDITION OR SITUATION:
Dealing with a Corrupt World

PRESCRIPTION:
Dead Souls (1842)
by Nikolai Gogol

*'I saw that I'd get nowhere on the straight path,
and that to go crookedly was straighter.'*

The stifling effects of bureaucracy have been discussed in relation to other books to live by, but whereas Franz Kafka discusses the isolation of identity and Joseph Heller the insanity of contradictory bureaucracy in relation to war, Gogol explores how bureaucracy can be riddled with systemic corruption.

Dead Souls is a satirical novel often considered one of the masterpieces of Russian literature. Set in provincial Russia during the early nineteenth century, the story follows Pavel Ivanovich Chichikov, a cunning and ambitious middle-aged man who travels through the countryside with a bizarre and morally dubious scheme. Chichikov seeks to purchase the ownership records of deceased serfs – referred to as 'souls' – who remain listed on the census rolls of landowners until the next official count. Since these 'dead souls' are still taxed as if they are alive, landowners are eager to offload them, and Chichikov acquires them at a low cost, planning to use the number of his non-existent serfs as collateral to secure loans and amass wealth. As he negotiates with a colourful cast of eccentric and often grotesque landowners, Chichikov's scheme unravels, exposing the absurdity, greed and moral decay of Russian society under the feudal system. One of Gogol's main aims is to highlight the inefficiencies and injustices of the serfdom system, portraying landowners as parasitic and detached from reality, and the bureaucracy as a tool for exploitation rather than governance.

Through the exaggerated and repulsive personalities of the characters – ranging from the miserly Plyushkin to the boastful Nozdryov – Gogol illustrates universal human vices such as vanity, laziness and dishonesty, suggesting these flaws underpin much of Russian society at that time.

Dead Souls, originally intended as a three-part epic but left incomplete at Gogol's death, combines dark humour with sharp social criticism, painting a vivid picture of human folly and systemic corruption.

Alternative Remedy:
Another novel that criticizes the system of serfdom in Russia in the nineteenth century and satirizes the fickleness and moral sloth of the land-owning aristocracy is *Oblomov* (1859) by Ivan Goncharov.

CONDITION OR SITUATION:
Facing the Horrors of Materialism

PRESCRIPTION:
Money (1984)
by Martin Amis

'Money doesn't mind if we say it's evil, it goes from strength to strength. It's a fiction, an addiction, and a tacit conspiracy.'

It's nice to have nice things, and having money is certainly preferable to not having money (see *Hunger* by Knut Hamsun). It is when the pursuit of materialist goods becomes all-encompassing and aspiration becomes avaricious and turns to greed that the soul becomes corrupted.

Martin Amis' novel *Money* explores these themes of materialism, greed and the corrupting influence of wealth. The story follows the life of John Self, a rich and successful film producer, immersed in the excesses of 1980s London. Self's actions are guided by his own self-interest, and he has no qualms about exploiting and manipulating others to get what he wants.

The novel is a satirical critique of the materialistic culture of the time, looking at the ways in which the pursuit of wealth and power can debase and destroy individuals, leading to a complete disregard for things that truly matter in life, such as ethics and morality.

As well as exploring the decline of moral values in modern society, Amis also looks at the illusion of social mobility and the ways in which the wealthy and powerful maintain their position and status. John Self's rise to wealth and success is a result of his own privilege and connections, rather than any genuine talent or hard work. Overall, *Money* suggests that materialism is a form of spiritual poverty.

Alternative Remedies:
The Bonfire of the Vanities (1987) by Tom Wolfe is a satirical novel that also explores the excesses of 1980s materialism but from an American perspective. For a much darker take on the horrors of materialism and moral bankruptcy, try *American Psycho* (1991) by Bret Easton Ellis.

CONDITION OR SITUATION:
Feeling Discontented with Life's Achievements

PRESCRIPTION:
Cannery Row (1945)
by John Steinbeck

'It has always seemed strange ... the things we admire in men, kindness and generosity, openness, honesty, understanding and feeling are the concomitants of failure in our system. And those traits we detest, sharpness, greed, acquisitiveness, meanness, egotism and self-interest are the traits of success. And while men admire the quality of the first, they love the produce of the second.'

Many people go through life feeling discontented with their lot. Perhaps one of the greatest tricks of consumer capitalism is that if you lived in a really nice house or could buy the latest gadgets, any gnawing feelings of discontentment would melt away into a bright new dawn of happy self-realization. Sadly, it almost certainly won't turn out that way.

The Stoic philosopher Marcus Aurelius (see Medicine Cabinet Essentials: *Meditations* by Marcus Aurelius) wrote: 'Do not dream of possession of what you do not have, rather reflect on the greatest blessings of what you do have.' In other words, take time out to reflect on aspects of your life that are positive, and count your blessings. This philosophy is beautifully evoked in John Steinbeck's novel *Cannery Row*.

This is not a novel in the conventional sense, but more a collection of loosely linked vignettes describing the denizens of a part of Monterey, California during the Great Depression. Steinbeck's characters, who are described unflatteringly as 'whores, pimps, gamblers and sons of bitches', are joined by a cheery group of unemployed hustlers, a migrant Chinese grocer/banker/landlord and a lonely marine biologist. What binds the characters together is a tacit acceptance of their lot. They live a hand-to-mouth existence but they survive by their wits and ingenuity, at the same time sharing values of mutual respect and solidarity. In many ways they are outliers, but they are free from the constraints and hollow values of mainstream society and exude *joie de vivre* in simple pleasures.

If ever you find yourself feeling disenchanted with the state of your life, pick up *Cannery Row* and read a few chapters and marvel at the funny, touching, life-affirming tales it contains.

Alternative Remedy:
For another dose of socially conscious stories from the underclass but with touches of magic realism, Turkish author Latife Tekin's novel *Berji Kristin: Tales from the Garbage Hills* (1984) describes the lives of squatters living in the slums on the outskirts of Istanbul in the 1980s.

CONDITION OR SITUATION:
Surviving Family Trauma

PRESCRIPTION:
Beloved (1987)
by Toni Morrison

'Freeing yourself was one thing, claiming ownership of that freed self was another.'

Few novels examine surviving family trauma quite so dramatically as this does. Depicting a mother's almost biblical journey towards healing and redemption, *Beloved* is a haunting and compelling novel that explores trauma, memory and the legacy of slavery. The story revolves around Sethe, a former slave who is haunted by the ghost of her dead daughter, whom she killed to save the child from a life of slavery.

The novel examines the ways in which traumatic experiences can be passed down through generations, affecting the lives of those who come after. Sethe's memories of slavery and her daughter's death are a constant presence, influencing her relationships and decisions. *Beloved* also explores the complexities of identity, particularly for African-Americans who have been displaced, enslaved and marginalized. Sethe and her family struggle to find a sense of belonging and identity in a world that has been hostile to them. Through the character of Sethe, Morrison suggests that healing and redemption are possible, but only by confronting the past and acknowledging the trauma that has been inflicted.

Although a harrowing and challenging book, *Beloved* ultimately offers up elements of hope and resilience, as well as examples of the enduring power of love that can help us overcome the traumas of the past.

Alternative Remedy:
The Brief Wondrous Life of Oscar Wao (2007) by Junot Díaz is a Pulitzer Prize-winning novel that tells the story of Oscar, a young Dominican–American man growing up in New Jersey, and his struggles with identity, culture and family history.

CONDITION OR SITUATION:
Supporting Others through Trauma

PRESCRIPTION:
A Little Life (2015)
by Hanya Yanagihara

*'How can you help someone who won't be helped
while realizing that if you don't try to help,
then you're not being a friend at all?'*

Childhood or adolescent traumas can have a crippling effect upon people's lives and relationships in adulthood, as revealed in this book. *A Little Life* is a sprawling and deeply emotional novel that follows the lives of four friends – Jude St Francis, Willem Ragnarsson, Malcolm Irvine and Jean-Baptist 'JB' Marion – over several decades, beginning with their college years at a prestigious university in Massachusetts and continuing through their adult lives in New York City. While the novel initially appears to be an ensemble story about friendship and ambition, it gradually narrows its focus to Jude, whose traumatic past and ongoing struggles with physical and emotional pain become the heart of the narrative.

Jude, a brilliant but enigmatic lawyer, is marked by a childhood of horrific abuse and abandonment. Orphaned as a baby, he endured years of physical, sexual and psychological torment at the hands of various so-called carers, first in a monastery and later through exploitative relationships, leaving him with permanent physical scars, chronic pain and severe emotional wounds. As an adult, Jude hides his past from even his closest friends, struggling with self-loathing, self-harm and an inability to accept love or happiness.

The novel's core theme is the enduring effect of childhood trauma on one's psyche and life. Jude's experiences of abuse shape every aspect of his existence – his self-worth, relationships and physical health – illustrating how trauma can become an indelible part of identity, often resisting even the most determined efforts at recovery.

A Little Life underscores the deep importance of bearing witness to someone's pain – listening, staying present and affirming their worth, as Willem does for Jude. For readers, this serves as a reminder that sometimes the most powerful act in the face of trauma and grief is simply to be there, offering an unconditional, safe space without any judgements, expectations or pressure.

Alternative Remedy:
The Great Believers (2018) by Rebecca Makkai covers similar themes as *A Little Life*, exploring the lives of three friends in Chicago at the height of the AIDS epidemic.

CONDITION OR SITUATION:
Losing Your Job

PRESCRIPTION:
Mr Phillips (2000)
by John Lanchester

'We wouldn't care so much what people thought of us if we knew how seldom they do.'

The sudden loss of a means of earning a living can be quite a shock, especially if it comes right out of the blue. For better or for worse, steady employment provides routine, structure and a degree of financial security, and to have that wrenched away can cause all manner of anxieties, from worries about money, fear of change and concerns for what the future may look like, to a creeping sense of failure and of being left 'on the scrap heap'.

John Lanchester's wry comic novel *Mr Phillips* explores the predicaments of sudden unemployment through the eyes and mind of a middle-aged accountant. Mr Phillips, too ashamed to tell his wife he has been made redundant, gets up the next day and pretends to go to work as usual. What follows is an odyssey around London during his usual working hours where he has several encounters and misadventures and ruminates on the meaning of his life up until this single day.

Mr Phillips is a slight book, full of understated ironies and dry, melancholy humour, but its message is simple: the world is a place of infinite possibilities and experiences that many people allow to pass them by until it is almost too late. Embracing uncertainty can be a liberating process!

Alternative Remedy:
For an alternative dose of a novel about a mid-life crisis and a sense of life wasted, *Less* (2017) by Andrew Sean Greer is a Pulitzer Prize-winning novel about the missteps and missed opportunities of a struggling, underachieving writer.

CONDITION OR SITUATION:
Living With Regret Over Missed Opportunities

PRESCRIPTION:
The Remains of the Day (1989)
by Kazuo Ishiguro

'Such evidently small incidents ... render whole dreams forever irredeemable.'

Few things haunt people more in the small hours than missed opportunities. Should the wasted prospect concern a matter of the heart, then spare a thought for Stevens, the central character in Kazuo Ishiguro's *The Remains of the Day*. A butler, Stevens has dedicated his life to serving the aristocratic Darlington family at their estate, Darlington Hall. The novel unfolds through Stevens' introspective narration when, in 1956, he embarks on a road trip to visit a former colleague, Miss Kenton, and reflects on his decades-long service to the family.

Stevens' story is characterized by his tendency to repress and deny his own emotions, desires and regrets. This repression is reflected in his avoidance of confrontation and his propensity to rationalize his decisions and actions.

The novel exposes the rigid social hierarchies of the time, as Stevens is bound by the conventions of his class and profession. His interactions with the aristocratic family and other servants are governed by strict rules of etiquette and protocol, which limit his ability to express himself or form genuine connections with others.

As Stevens reflects on his life, he is forced to confront the passage of time and the choices he has made. He begins to realize that his dedication to his duty has come at a great personal cost, and that he has missed out on opportunities for love, friendship and personal growth. The novel reminds us that time is a finite resource, and that our choices and actions have consequences that can shape the course of our lives.

The Remains of the Day explores the complexities and nuances of human relationships, highlighting the ways in which our interactions with others can be marked by both love and regret, connection and disconnection.

Alternative Remedy:
The pain of regret is examined in Matt Haig's philosophical fantasy novel *The Midnight Library* (2020), which tells the story of a suicidal thirty-five-year-old woman who finds herself in a state of limbo between life and death, reliving all the choices she has made throughout her life.

List of Books and Authors

---◆---

Achebe, Chinua, *Things Fall Apart*, p. 198
Alcott, Louisa May, *Little Women*, p. 192
Amis, Martin, *Money*, p. 208
Andrić, Ivo, *The Bridge on the Drina*, p. 182
Angelou, Maya, *I Know Why the Caged Bird Sings*, p. 64
Armah, Ayi Kwei, *The Beautyful Ones Are Not Yet Born*, p. 154
Atwood, Margaret, *The Handmaid's Tale*, p. 158
Aurelius, Marcus, *Meditations*, p. 84
Austen, Jane, *Pride and Prejudice*, p. 140
Bach, Richard, *Jonathan Livingston Seagull*, p. 100
Baldwin, James, *Go Tell It on the Mountain*, p. 58
Beckett, Samuel, *Murphy*, p. 96
de Bernières, Louis, *Captain Corelli's Mandolin*, p. 40
Bond, Ruskin, *The Blue Umbrella*, p. 200
Brontë, Charlotte, *Jane Eyre*, p. 164
Brontë, Emily, *Wuthering Heights*, p. 32
Bulgakov, Mikhail, *The Master and Margarita*, p. 12
Camus, Albert, *The Outsider*, p. 92
Carson, Anne, *The Beauty of the Husband*, p. 20
Carver, Raymond, *What We Talk About When We Talk About Love*, p. 76

Cather, Willa, *My Ántonia*, p. 48
de Cervantes, Miguel, *Don Quixote*, p. 204
Choderlos de Laclos, Pierre, *Les Liaisons Dangereuses*, p. 52
Coelho, Paolo, *The Alchemist*, p. 88
Coetzee, J. M., *The Life and Times of Michael K*, p. 120
Conrad, Joseph, *Heart of Darkness*, p. 102
Dangarembga, Tsitsi, *Nervous Conditions*, p. 146
Dickens, Charles, *Great Expectations*, p. 152
Dostoevsky, Fyodor, *Crime and Punishment*, p. 98
Eco, Umberto, *The Name of the Rose*, p. 70
van Eeden, Frederik, *The Quest*, p. 62
Eliot, George, *Middlemarch*, p. 34
Faulkner, William, *As I Lay Dying*, p. 118
Fitzgerald, F. Scott, *The Great Gatsby*, p. 46
Flaubert, Gustave, *Madame Bovary*, p. 38
Ford, Ford Maddox, *The Good Soldier*, p. 36
Forster, E. M., *A Room with a View*, p. 16
Fowles, John, *The Magus*, p. 104
Frank, Anne, *The Diary of a Young Girl*, p. 178
García Márquez, Gabriel, *Love in the Time of Cholera*, p. 28
von Goethe, Johann Wolfgang, *The Sorrows of Young Werther*, p. 14
Gogol, Nikolai, *Dead Souls*, p. 206
Grass, Günter, *The Tin Drum*, p. 124
Greene, Graham, *The Power and the Glory*, p. 56
Hamsun, Knut, *Hunger*, p. 94
Hartley, L. P., *The Go-Between*, p. 50
Heller, Joseph, *Catch-22*, p. 126
Hemingway, Ernest, *The Old Man and the Sea*, p. 150

Hesse, Hermann, *Siddhartha*, p. 60
Hurston, Zora Neale, *Their Eyes Were Watching God*, p. 170
Ishiguro, Kazuo, *The Remains of the Day*, p. 218
Kadare, Ismail, *The General of the Dead Army*, p. 116
Kafka, Franz, *The Trial*, p. 186
Kang, Han, *The White Book*, p. 72
Kawaguchi, Toshikazu, *Before the Coffee Gets Cold*, p. 86
Kazantzakis, Nikos, *Zorba the Greek*, p. 190
Keneally, Thomas, *Schindler's List*, p. 168
Kerouac, Jack, *On the Road*, p. 196
Kesey, Ken, *One Flew Over the Cuckoo's Nest*, p. 128
Kundera, Milan, *The Unbearable Lightness of Being*, p. 66
Lanchester, John, *Mr Phillips*, p. 216
Lee, Harper, *To Kill a Mockingbird*, p. 136
Levi, Primo, *If This Is a Man*, p. 142
McEwan, Ian, *Enduring Love*, p. 42
Mann, Thomas, *The Magic Mountain*, p. 180
Martel, Yann, *Life of Pi*, p. 78
Morrison, Toni, *Beloved*, p. 212
Müller, Herta, *The Hunger Angel*, p. 80
Murakami, Haruki, *Norwegian Wood*, p. 148
Murdoch, Iris, *The Sea, The Sea*, p. 132
Nabokov, Vladimir, *Lolita*, p. 112
Natthiko Lindeblad, Björn, *I May Be Wrong*, p. 68
Norwood, Robin, *Women Who Love Too Much*, p. 22
O'Brien, Edna, *The Country Girls*, p. 160
O'Farrell, Maggie, *After You'd Gone*, p. 74
Pamuk, Orhan, *The Museum of Innocence*, p. 44
Pârvulescu, Ioana, *Life Begins on Friday*, p. 82

Pavić, Milorad, *Last Love in Constantinople*, p. 176
Pirsig, Robert M., *Zen and the Art of Motorcycle Maintenance*, p. 106
Pynchon, Thomas, *The Crying of Lot 49*, p. 114
Rooney, Sally, *Conversations with Friends*, p. 18
Roth, Philip, *American Pastoral*, p. 184
Roy, Arundhati, *The God of Small Things*, p. 194
Rushdie, Salman, *Midnight's Children*, p. 108
Salinger, J. D., *The Catcher in the Rye*, p. 138
Sartre, Jean-Paul, *Nausea*, p. 130
Seth, Vikram, *A Suitable Boy*, p. 188
Shikibu, Murasaki, *The Tale of Genji*, p. 30
Solzhenitsyn, Aleksandr, *One Day in the Life of Ivan Denisovich*, p. 156
Sōseki Natsume, *I Am a Cat*, p. 202
Steinbeck, John, *Cannery Row*, p. 210
Tartt, Donna, *The Secret History*, p. 122
Tolstoy, Leo, *Anna Karenina*, p. 24
Twain, Mark, *Adventures of Huckleberry Finn*, p. 166
Vonnegut, Kurt, *Slaughterhouse-Five*, p. 110
Walker, Alice, *The Color Purple*, p. 162
Waugh, Evelyn, *A Handful of Dust*, p. 26
Wharton, Edith, *The Age of Innocence*, p. 172
Yanagihara, Hanya, *A Little Life*, p. 214
Zola, Émile, *Germinal*, p. 144